Examining What We Do to Improve Our Schools

8 Steps From Analysis to Action

Sandra Harris
Stacey Edmonson
Julie Combs

EYE ON EDUCATION
6 DEPOT WAYWEST, SUITE 106
LARCHMONT, NY 10538
(914) 833–0551
(914) 833–0761 fax
www.eyeoneducation.com

A sincere effort has been made to supply the identity of those who have created
specific strategies. Any omissions have been unintentional.

Library of Congress Cataloging-in-Publication Data

Harris, Sandra, 1946-
   Examining what we do to improve our schools : 8 steps from analysis
to action / by Sandra Harris, Stacey Edmonson, Julie P. Combs.
        p. cm.
   Includes bibliographical references.
   ISBN 978-1-59667-135-5
   1. School improvement programs--Planning. 2. Educational
leadership. I. Edmonson, Stacey. II. Combs, Julie P. III. Title.
   LB2822.8.H375 2009
   371.2'07--dc22

                                                                      2009032156

10 9 8 7 6 5 4 3 2

Production services provided by
Rick Soldin a Book Production Specialist
Jonesborough, TN — www.book-comp.com

Also Available from Eye On Education

Meet the Authors

Sandra Harris is Professor and Director of the Center for Doctoral Studies in Educational Leadership at Lamar University in Beaumont, Texas, where she teaches courses in social justice and qualitative research. Formerly, she served as a teacher, principal, and superintendent in public and private schools. Her scholarship agenda includes administrator preparation and building relationship-oriented, socially-just school environments. She has authored or co-authored over 100 journal articles and book chapters as well as 15 books including *BRAVO Teacher*, *BRAVO Principal*, and *Managing Conflict: 50 Strategies for School Leaders*. She presents at regional, state, and national conferences on these and other related topics, in addition to consulting with school districts.

Stacey L. Edmonson is Professor and Director of the Center for Research and Doctoral Studies in Educational Leadership at Sam Houston State University in Huntsville, Texas, where she teaches courses in qualitative research, instructional theory, and school law. Formerly, she has been a central office administrator, principal, and teacher in Texas public schools. Her research interests include stress and burnout among educators, legal issues in education, and educator ethics. She has authored several books and articles and presents at regional, state, and national conferences on these and other related topics, in addition to consulting with school districts.

Julie P. Combs is currently Assistant Professor of Educational Leadership at Sam Houston State University. Prior to her position in higher education, she served as a campus principal for 10 years. She has given over 75 international, national, state, and local presentations, one-half of which include consultations with schools and districts. She has published numerous journal articles, book chapters, and co-authored the book, *Managing Conflict: 50 Strategies for School Leaders*. Her current research interests include trust and leadership, the roles and duties of principals, and leadership burnout.

Free Downloads

The tools discussed and displayed in this book are also available on Eye On Education's website as Adobe Acrobat files. Permission has been granted to purchasers of this book to download these tools and print them.

You can access these downloads by visiting Eye On Education's website: **www.eyeoneducation.com**.

Click on **FREE Downloads** or search or browse our website to find this book and then scroll down for downloading instructions.

You'll need your bookbuyer access code: EXA-7135-5

List of Free Downloads

Contents

Introduction

Educators are busier than ever before. Research has documented that responsibilities of superintendents, principals, and teachers continue to expand both in scope and in number. The job is not getting easier! If leaders accept the challenge, then they need to foster a leadership culture where the process of examining the work for school improvement is a continual shared responsibility of the campus and larger community. This process must be embedded in all of the work of the school, whether it is hiring faculty, monitoring curriculum, testing for academic achievement, teaching students, or meeting any other educational need.

Because of the challenge for continual improvement, formal improvement processes capture the attention of many educators at all levels—public and private schools, colleges, and universities. Improvement plans and the groups of individuals that write and evaluate them are referred to by a variety of names and acronyms and include accrediting agencies, such as the Southern Association of Colleges and Schools (SACS). Many accrediting agencies require improvement processes, peer-evaluation, and self-regulation. In addition, each of the 50 state departments of education requires improvement planning as a method to meet state and federal standards (e.g., No Child Left Behind Act of 2001 [NCLB]).

Campus or district improvement is often planned and conducted through the collaborative efforts of people in and around the school, at least in theory. Sometimes, in practice, only a few individuals create and submit the plan, giving superficial attention to the improvement committee and/or collaboration and improvement. At the same time, school leaders are expected to facilitate improvement with their teachers and students result ing in success that is sometimes narrowly defined by student performance on annual exams. In addition, school leaders are often told exactly WHAT and HOW improvement must occur. In doing so, many school leaders have lost sight of authentic school improvement. As former administrators, we believe that a campus-specific improvement process is critical to the health of a school and the welfare of its students and believe that leaders want to facilitate a genuine improvement that unifies the school community. This book is written for school leaders who want to:

- ◆ Engage in meaningful improvement in their schools

- ◆ Empower their teachers to willingly and collectively participate in improvement

- ◆ Broaden the definitions of performance indicators

- ◆ Understand the skills and tools necessary to lead effective change.

We as authors hope that, by the end of this book, you will understand how to make improvement a genuine process and how to use these plans to transform your organization.

An improvement is "something that enhances value or excellence" (Merriam-Webster, 2008), so an improvement plan is a written document that ideally results in enhancement and excellence. Change is sometimes mistaken for improvement. Change means to make different, to replace, or to exchange. Therefore, change is not necessarily improvement. Often, new programs bring about change, but this does not always mean that they result in genuine improvement. Therefore, we make the distinction that doing something differently is not necessarily doing something better.

To improve schools, leaders should focus on the work to improve schools on a continual basis of discovery. Discovery is rarely about creating something new, but is most likely about seeing what was already there with a new understanding. Examining the work means that leaders will ask questions, such as *why, who, when, how,* and *what if* for the goal of improving their schools. Columbus did not start out to "discover" America at all. He began by wondering, "Is there a quicker way to sail to the West Indies?" By trying to answer that inquiry, he found a land that was already there and "discovered" America! Einstein did not discover the theory of relativity. Yet, looking at energy in different ways, he "discovered" an understanding of energy that already existed. How did Ben Franklin discover electricity? How did Thomas Edison discover how to make sound travel through a wire to become a telephone? How was penicillin discovered? Examining the work and asking questions can provide data, which ultimately might lead to school improvement.

Too often leaders focus on the problem of the moment and only *begin* to approach an effective examination of the work. This happens when leaders have a limited understanding of assessment as answering questions to solve a problem—the means to an end. However, true examination, or looking at the work to improve schools, leads to something much greater than seeking an answer to a problem. Leaders must develop a state of mind that realizes that discovery of an answer to one problem leads to the next question and on to the next question—ultimately leading to deeper and richer information. Examination of the work is not about just finding *the right solution* to a problem. It is about asking the *right questions* to understand the problem. In other words, it is *problem solving* based on *problem understanding*.

Figure 1

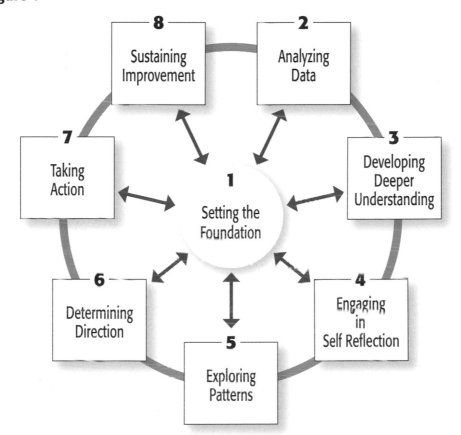

Other books and resources are available that cover the subject of school improvement. Some are idealistic, some are technical, and some explain specific skills such as how to analyze data. What makes this book different is that in addition to our unique explanation and application of examining the work that leads to school improvement, we, as authors, begin with an often assumed part of the process—the foundational beliefs and attention to inter-personal relationships that ultimately facilitate or hinder progress. Although one can apply the skills of improvement, the underlying beliefs signal the difference between a genuinely authentic improvement experience and one that is conducted with the primary goal of just getting it done, "checking the box," and moving on to the next issue.

Today, leaders of schools are expected to improve their schools. They are required to gather and analyze data, submit written improvement plans, and implement these ideas with the cooperation of other faculty members and the community. As authors and former administrators, we believe that an improvement plan should be a genuine process that ultimately has mean-ing and value for those involved. It is this challenge of understanding that allows the process of examining the work of schools to result in actions that lead to improved schools. We outline a process, as shown in Figure 1, with 8 critical action steps: setting the foundation, analyzing data, developing deeper understanding, engaging in self-reflection, exploring programmatic patterns, determining direction, taking action, and sustaining improvements. These action steps provide a framework for examining school improvement that is an ongoing thoughtful evaluation of the work. We believe that when this framework is implemented, schools can be improved.

You may be reading this book because you want to improve your school and need more ideas. Perhaps your organization and its reputation are in jeopardy because test scores were lower than expected. Maybe you would like to become more familiar with the improvement process and need infor-mation on how to lead such a process. Whatever the reason, we believe that you will benefit from thinking about the ideas presented in this book. We, as former school and district leaders, have applied these ideas in our own organizations with positive results.

This book shows school leaders how they can infuse their daily practice with an examination of the actions they take to improve their schools. It identifies 8 steps that inform the school improvement process and boost student achievement. The chapters are organized around the Framework for Examining School Improvement. Strategies to use with school commu-nities are provided as a guide for school leaders to examine their work and identify appropriate actions that improve schools. Each chapter includes a Summing Up section, a statement to remember, reflection questions, and one or more resources. We believe that when busy leaders embed these 8 action steps in examining the work on their campuses, improved schools will result.

Step 1
Examining the Work: Setting the Foundation

We must exchange the philosophy of excuse for the philosophy of responsibility.
Barbara Jordan, U.S. Congresswoman

We aren't where we want to be, we aren't where we ought to be, but thank goodness, we aren't where we used to be.
Lou Holtz, NCAA Football and NFL head coach

The Framework for Examining School Improvement depicted in Figure 1 outlines 8 steps to improve an organization. The process is cyclical and continuous. In the first step, Setting the Foundation forms the basis for all improvement activity. Some will label concepts in this step as "good leadership," others will say that this foundation includes dispositions, attitudes, or states of mind. Completion of each step in the Framework builds on the work of previous steps. For example, the tasks in Step 2, Analyzing Data, are used to develop deeper understanding in Step 3. The analysis activities of Steps 2 through 4 are used to explore patterns in Step 5. All of this information is then used to determine a direction in Step 6 and to take action in Step 7. The necessary time to complete each step varies by the topic, the size of the group, and the data available. Ideally, an organization would complete the cycle in an academic year. Previous efforts and results would be used to inform the next cycle to sustain improvement, as outlined in Step 8.

Although the Framework for Examining School Improvement appears to be straightforward, leading and doing the work of improvement can be challenging. However, many barriers impede school improvement efforts such as limited resources, lack of support from central office or the school board, and pressures from special interest groups. The impact of barriers is lessened when the foundation for school improvement is in place. We believe that four of the more common barriers for school leaders, once identified, can be resolved. These four barriers are (a) the lack of a shared vision, (b) the lack of understanding the need for inquiry, (c) the lack of valuing improvement by not providing time for improvement, and (d) the lack of trust among teachers, administrators, students, and parents. Therefore, having a shared vision, understanding the need for inquiry, valuing improvement by providing time, and building interpersonal trust are essential to establishing a strong foundation for examining the work for school improvement.

Having a Shared Vision

Organizations need leaders who understand that their role in the school improvement process begins with understanding the need to have a shared vision. Bennis and Goldsmith (1997) stated it well when they wrote that the first role of any leader is to "create a compelling vision that takes people to a new place, and to translate that vision into action" (p. 4). Leithwood and Jantzi (2005) called this setting direction. School leaders understand that there are many ways to improve schools, but it is absolutely vital that everyone know and agree upon the basic direction. Whether we call this a shared vision, shared mission, or shared goal is irrelevant. What is important is that individuals in an organization agree in order to work collaboratively with the same end goal in mind.

Several years ago, one of us surveyed 123 teachers about what their principals did to promote a positive school climate that supported teacher quality and student learning. All of the teachers listed the importance of being able to participate in identifying and clarifying the school vision as one of their principal's actions. However, one in four teachers listed this as the single most important act of their principal! Although involving faculty members in identifying the vision for the school is important, school leaders also need to involve staff, students, and the larger community in creating this shared vision. Remember, having a shared vision is foundational before genuine school improvement can occur.

In order to involve the faculty, staff, and other stakeholders in participating in identifying a shared vision for the school, time must be set aside to reflect and discuss questions, such as the following:

◆ What do I consider the school's image to be in my own mind?

◆ What do others who work at the school consider the school's image to be?

◆ What do students consider the school's image to be?

◆ What does the community consider the school's image to be?

◆ What should the school's role be for students?

◆ What should the school's role be for the community?

◆ What unique contribution to the students and the community can only be made by the school?

◆ What do we value?

◆ How do we communicate these values?

◆ What goals should be set to move the school as an organization toward fulfilling what we value as our collective shared vision?

Framing the school's vision around student success is essential. School leaders who acknowledge the importance of having a shared vision for their school framed around student success have pointed out that many times a day they ask the following questions of themselves, faculty and other stakeholders regarding the activities of the school:

- What is our collective shared vision?

- How does this activity help us achieve our collective school vision?

- In what way might this activity be a barrier to achieving our collective school vision?

- Is there a way to re-evaluate what we are doing to achieve our shared goal?

As important as it is for school leaders to involve faculty and others in creating the school vision, it becomes equally important to continuously remind everyone of that vision. Therefore, the vision is shared on two levels: (a) shared among faculty in the form of common values, and (b) communicated or shared to others on a regular basis.

When there is no shared vision in place, a major barrier is constructed which does not allow for genuine school improvement. By involving everyone in the process of creating a shared vision, this barrier is removed, and it is possible to engage in understanding the need for inquiry, which is the next essential component for providing a foundation on which genuine school improvement can occur.

Understanding the Need for Inquiry

Once a shared vision is agreed upon and is communicated, it is necessary to understand that the need for inquiry is an essential component in order to establish a firm foundation for school improvement. What is inquiry? Inquiry is investigating in a systematic way. Inquiry is examining data, asking questions, and requesting more information. The inquiry process, based on logical reasoning, requires the collection of information in a systematic way.

You may be familiar with inquiry as a teaching strategy or method of investigation. For example, inquiry supports the scientific process. Because inquiry involves reasoning and processing, teachers have been encouraged to model inquiry by verbalizing the thinking process for students (e.g., metacognitive strategies). There are teaching methods based on inquiry such as inquiry-based learning, inquiry-based teaching, and problem-based learning. For some, inquiry simply means to ask questions. For us as authors, inquiry is the process of thinking and questioning that undergirds the Framework for Examining School Improvement.

To illustrate the concepts of inquiry and improvement planning in a simple way, consider an example related to a high-performing school principal's health. For several months, she did not feel well physically and continued to get sick, especially during weekends and breaks. She reasoned that she was just as busy (and tired) as other school administrators working 60+ hour weeks. This continued until one day a friend commented on her declining health; she realized that she was not improving. Reluctantly, she made an appointment with a doctor who was highly respected. At the appointment, the doctor listened, asked questions, and ordered various diagnostic tests. Based on the results, the doctor ruled out possibilities and ordered additional tests. He continued through this process of reviewing information and asking more questions until he had enough data to render a diagnosis. After sharing the diagnosis with her, the doctor developed a plan of action in the form of a prescription, which included medication, diet, exercise, and stress reduction strategies. Follow-up visits and repeated tests guided the direction of the administrator's personal improvement plan over several months. After a year, her condition improved and she transitioned into a maintenance phase, which included long-term lifestyle changes.

Although simplistic, the process used to improve the administrator's health aligns to the Framework for Examining School Improvement. Having a shared vision, understanding the need for inquiry, valuing the time involved, and trusting her physician (Setting the Foundation), she agreed to participate in an examination of her health. She and the doctor then worked through Step 2, Analyzing Data (the data were her described symptoms), and Step 3, Developing Deeper Understanding, which involved ordering diagnostic tests. The doctor used a combination of data types and sources such as her verbalized symptoms, past medical records and assessments, and diagnostic tests. Next, the doctor engaged in self-reflection guided by his experience and training, which was Step 4 and Step 5, Exploring Patterns. After combining all the information, he proceeded to Step 6, Determining a Direction. Next, he designed a plan of action (the prescriptions and his notes) and scheduled future appointments to monitor and evaluate the plan, which is the essence of Step 7, Taking Action for Improvement. During monitoring visits, new information was used to refine and continue the improvement process. When the administrator's progress eventually reached acceptable levels, she transitioned into a maintenance phase (Step 8, Sustaining Improvement), which included annual diagnostics and continued attention to lifestyle choices.

Thankfully, doctors are trained to use a systematic approach to improvement based on the process of inquiry and use of diagnostic data from multiple sources. The diagnostic data are typically not the results/scores from just one test. Rather, test results and other quantitative measures (e.g., blood work, blood pressure) are combined with the patient's input and doctor's notes from past visits (qualitative data). The combination or use of mixed data sources can provide a more accurate and meaningful picture and consequently lead to a better decision and successful solution.

Valuing Improvement by Providing Time for Improvement

How frequently have you heard someone say, "There is not enough time to (fill in the blank)" or "There are only 24 hours in a day"? A common barrier to effective and genuine examination of the work that leads to school improvement is the lack of time. Specifically, barriers exist for progress when educators fail to allot enough time to plan and do improvement. Some school leaders believe they are too busy for planning. Some lack the skills related to effective planning such as projecting, scheduling, budgeting, and communicating. Some do not see the value in examining improvement efforts and will not spare the time for self and group reflection. The initial steps in the improvement process take time, patience, thought, and reflection. Rushing through these steps can produce superficial activities, characterized by "all show and no substance."

To illustrate this common lack of planning, consider the case of the technology director who was asked by the superintendent to develop a technology improvement plan for the district's schools. Because the superintendent felt pressured by school board members to present a recommendation at the next meeting, she gave the technology director less than 2 weeks to develop a plan. (Wait, I bet you can finish this story!) Although the technology director believed in the importance of teacher and administrator input, he based the plan on the ideas of a few principals and one convincing salesperson. Unfortunately, the schools ended up with equipment that frequented the storage closets and a technology director who frequented job-posting sites!

As career educators, we have survived numerous projects, new programs, and changes "dressed up" as improvement. With few exceptions, the efforts that have produced the best results were afforded time and careful analysis in their initial stages. Because of pressing deadlines and urgent responsibilities, improvement planning can be an activity that is pushed aside or postponed. Although important, this process is not viewed as urgent, so finding time for examining the improvement planning can be one of the greatest barriers to progress.

Building Interpersonal Trust

Lack of trust is another barrier to genuinely examining the work in school improvement. High trust within a school increases the chances that school reform and implementation will take place. What is trust, exactly? Someone once said, "Trust is like air; we don't notice it until it is polluted" (author unknown). Trust, like air, is a complex interchange of many elements. Trust involves the balance of several invisible qualities such as being reliable, competent, respectful, honest, and open (Bennis, 1999; Bryk & Schneider, 2002). For example, think about an organization, a team, or a job where you experienced high trust. How would you describe the team's levels of productivity or success? What characterized the relationships with your coworkers?

Generally, individuals in high-trust organizations experience higher levels of productivity and job satisfaction than do those in low-trust organizations. Organizations that are characterized by high trust can face challenges more effectively because their energy and focus are reserved for solving the "real" problems. On the other hand, organizations with low trust have more problems related to issues of power, control, and communication. People in low-trust environments experience the same problems differently than those in high-trust situations do, primarily because of the interpersonal relationships. As such, interpersonal challenges and problem solving relate directly to the work of school improvement.

How people get information and share information differs in high-trust versus low-trust situations. Lack of trust often couples with an increased attempt to control, which influences communication. Typically, leaders in low-trust organizations share less information in general. Instead, information is shared with selected individuals, typically those who are favored. Hence, the informal grapevine serves as the main information source for the members. Although the grapevine exists in all organizations, differences occur in the types of information shared. In low-trust environments, the grapevine serves as a primary communication method and carries information that is somewhat reliable. In high-trust situations, essential information is shared with everyone through methods that are more formal, and the grapevine is used to convey mostly social and interpersonal news.

Moreover, in low-trust situations people take fewer risks. Much of the dialogue among coworkers occurs *after* meetings rather than *in* meetings, and this phenomenon has been called the *parking lot effect*. Individuals with ideas different from those in charge may be ostracized, embarrassed, and ignored. As such, all members may be reluctant to contribute. If dissenting points of view are presented, individuals with dissenting ideas can be seen as unsupportive, critical, and negative. Typically, the ideas of one or a few are seen as superior to all others; thus, dialogue is not necessary. The limited dialogue and the secretive nature of low-trust organizations counter the conditions needed to examine data and generate solutions in the improvement process. Unfortunately, bad decisions have been made because of the conditions present in low-trust environments, including impatience and an unwillingness to accept alternative ideas.

How do you take "trust readings" in your organization? Here are some questions that you might want to consider:

- ◆ To what extent does the leader listen and observe?

- ◆ In meetings, how are new ideas presented? How are those individuals sharing the ideas received?

- ◆ Is the sharing of new ideas encouraged or silenced?

- ◆ In the general areas of the school, how do adults talk to the students?

- ◆ Does the leader follow specific routines and procedures to increase efficiency and offer a sense of security?

- ◆ Is there a sense of order in the school?

- ◆ Does the leader demonstrate congruence between his/her words and actions?

- ◆ Are promises kept?

Leaders should question the alignment of words and actions as a way to improve trust-building actions. In addition, leaders need to pay attention to perceptions and provide accurate and frequent communication to counter the effects of misinformation. These are many other strategies for building trust, which are detailed in a variety of books on the subject.

A second way to assess the trust between the leader and the staff is to distribute an anonymous questionnaire, which can be found in Tool 1.1. However, keep in mind that soliciting input is not for the faint of heart. If you use this tool, make sure you want to know the answers before you ask the questions! Specifically, how you handle the results of questionnaires will demonstrate your levels of trustworthiness. People will "read" your reaction and determine how open they can be with you in the future. If the respondents predict the possibility of a negative reaction, some will be dishonest and inflate their answers and others will not respond at all. Therefore, in

Tool 1.1 Trust Inventory

Please take a moment to consider the extent to which each statement below describes your feelings about the trust you feel with the leaders in this school. The feedback from all respondents will be summarized and used for improvement purposes. Please provide information that will be helpful. You will remain anonymous unless you choose to identify yourself. Use the following scale: 1 – Rarely; 2 – Sometimes; 3 – Usually; 4 – Always

The leader	Rarely	Sometimes	Usually	Always
1. Takes an interest in me as a person.	1	2	3	4
2. Follows through with commitments.	1	2	3	4
3. Is ethical.	1	2	3	4
4. Keeps his/her word.	1	2	3	4
5. Listens to the suggestions of others.	1	2	3	4
6. Is open to suggestions and new ideas.	1	2	3	4
7. Is competent.	1	2	3	4
8. Is a good listener.	1	2	3	4
9. Expects others to display respectful behavior.	1	2	3	4
10. Addresses others in a respectful tone.	1	2	3	4
11. Cares about my professional development.	1	2	3	4
12. Is consistent in what he/she says and does.	1	2	3	4

Please describe your thoughts for the following questions:

How would you describe the trust levels among staff members in our school?

How would you describe trust levels between staff members and administrators in this school?

low-trust organizations, honest feedback is uncommon and rarely is received in a way that results in meaningful improvement. So, if honest feedback abounds in your organization, congratulations! Open dialogue and honest feedback are indicators of high trust.

Organizing Structures for School Improvement

Along with having a shared vision giving value to the work of school improvement and providing time for such efforts, a system to organize the work is also part of establishing the foundation. We advocate the forming of workgroups using a schoolwide improvement committee along with subcommittees. This committee structure will require that staff members participate actively in continuous improvement efforts. To begin, you will need to establish a schoolwide committee with approximately 8 to 12 members who will agree to serve as committee leaders. Your state or local educational agency may already require such a committee, particularly in light of states legislating site-based decision-making and consensus-building processes for schools. If you do not have an established leadership team or some type of school planning committee, consider creating such a committee. Although it may seem logical to appoint existing department heads or grade-level leaders to the committees, consider the teacher-leadership opportunities that can be afforded to other staff members. Sometimes teachers and staff have elected these members and/or the principal has appointed individuals.

Staff members appointed or elected to the improvement committee will then be asked to lead or co-lead a subcommittee consisting of a small group of teachers, with groups ranging in size from 3 to 12 members. To be successful, these subcommittee leaders will need initial and refresher trainings in group leadership skills. Such topics could include agenda planning, communication, conflict management, and consensus-building strategies. School leaders can use this structure to build leadership capacity among their teachers

At a minimum, the improvement committee will need to meet at least once every 6 to 8 weeks. If this schoolwide committee will address other concerns besides improvement activities, then additional meetings may be needed. Ideally, the subcommittees led by members of the core improvement team will meet at least once a quarter and sometimes more, depending on the activities they lead. School administrators and teachers may be challenged finding the time to meet. One strategy that works is to provide time for these groups to meet during a 20- to 30-minute segment at monthly faculty meetings and during a 1- to 2-hour period within a staff inservice day. For best results, the principal or designated school leader will need to plan the committees and the meeting dates in advance. By sharing the lists of committee assignments, meeting dates, and expected outcomes at the beginning of the year, the leader communicates the importance of ensuring that improvement will occur.

The involvement of parents, students, and other school community members on the improvement committee or subcommittees, although proposed in theory, can be challenging in practice. Often, the committee meeting times are not convenient for parents or community members. Moreover, these groups, including student representatives, may lose interest or feel unequipped to provide any real assistance to the process of planning and carrying out the details. From experience, we suggest that you find a way to involve parents, community members, and students and reserve two or more positions on the schoolwide committee for their representation.

Next, consider what these various groups could offer to the goals of school improvement. For example, they may share unique perspectives that broaden understanding of the entire committee, or they may be aware of available resources. Parents or community members may have the time and a desire to help organize or carry out some of the activities. To enhance the involvement of parents, students, and community members who will serve on the committee, schedule a time to explain to them the school improvement process and the steps of the Framework for Examining School Improvement. Invite them to attend a session when your staff will be analyzing data explained in Chapter 2. Think of ways to involve them in the process and use their unique perspectives. Provide them with an invitation and a calendar of future meetings of the improvement committee, but allow them to opt out of regular attendance if their schedules do not permit. Even so, include them in communication regarding the work of the committee. If they cannot attend meetings, you can ask their opinions by way of informal conversations or electronic communication. Undoubtedly, the perspectives of students and parents can help improvement efforts be more effective and supported.

Although there are many benefits, involving parents, community members, and even students can be a risk. A focus on examination and improvement might imply weakness. Moreover, principals know that positive public relations are vital. Often, leaders invest much thought and time when managing perceptions. Still, parents, students, and community members, well informed, can be some of the most credible supporters as they often have the most accurate information. Should you feel reluctant to involve members outside of your staff, start small, and invest time to explain and communicate how your school examines its work. Most reasonable parents, students, and community members will respect your efforts and conclude that your staff is committed to doing what is best.

Summing Up

In this chapter, we discussed the first step in the Framework for Examining School Improvement, Setting the Foundation. Setting the foundation emphasizes having a shared vision, understanding the need for inquiry, valuing the provision of time for improvement, and building interpersonal trust. In addition, a practical system is offered for establishing a structure to support improvement efforts. Before you move to the chapters focused on the other 7 steps in the framework, consider the foundation established in your school. An organization that values the improvement process and operates with high levels of trust will approach problem solving in a manner that truly improves the school. Wherever you find educators genuinely engaged in examining the work they do to improve schools, you will find evidence of sharing a vision understanding the need for inquiry, valuing investments of time, and building interpersonal trust.

Remember:
Establishing the foundation is essential for genuine improvement to occur and requires having a shared vision, understanding the need for inquiry, valuing improvement by investing time, and building interpersonal trust.

Reflection Questions:

1. Considering your experiences, what are some examples of change that did not result in improvement?

2. What standards or processes are used to accredit or rate your organization? What are the requirements for improvement planning in your school?

3. Combining multiple data sources can lead to more accurate and meaningful conclusions. What are your thoughts about this concept?

4. What, if any, have been your experiences with examining school improvement processes?

5. How do you know that your organization has a shared vision?

6. How do you know that your organization understands the need for inquiry?

7. How much time has been allotted for improvement?

8. How is the process for improvement structured?

9. What have been the results of improvement plans and actions?

10. How would you rate the trust levels in your current work environment?

Step 2
Examining the Work: Analyzing Data

We learn more by looking for the answer to a question and not finding it than we do learning the answer itself.

Lloyd Alexander, author

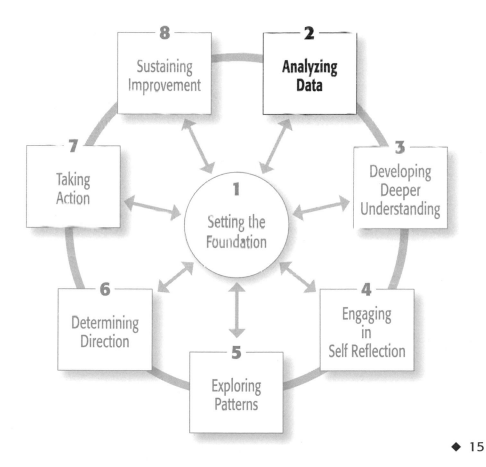

Using data to make decisions has been a popular topic for educators for the past several years. Claims of decisions that are "data-driven" and programs that are "evidence-based" have proliferated educational literature to the point of becoming trite and even insincere. Data exist in large quantities for those who work in schools. Yet, it has been said that educators are *data rich* but *information poor*, otherwise known as DRIPs, for short! The Framework for Examining School Improvement can help schools become rich in information too. Now that we have discussed Step 1 in the framework and have established the foundation, it is time to discuss Step 2, Analyzing Data.

Monovision Analysis

Receiving test score reports is a regular occurrence for most district and campus leaders. Within the current context of public accountability, expected standards, and sanctions for unfavorable scores, the actual receipt of these high-stakes test results can induce both anticipation and alarm for the most fearless of leaders. Leaders' reactions vary; some hurry to determine if expected goals were achieved, and others delegate the review to another staff member and wait for a report of good or bad news. We have known building principals who, after receiving their school's score reports, go into hiding for a few hours in order to digest the facts, anticipating an onset of questions from their supervisors, school board members, and the media.

Although these score reports offer a plethora of information, data analysis is much more than a review of one test. Believing that one test serves as *the* performance indicator for a school is shortsighted, resulting in missed opportunities to celebrate other strengths and to identify areas of need. Such an attitude may diminish the extent to which schools may examine their work. Even when important external critics (district leaders, the community, the media) emphasize this one performance indicator, the school leader, demonstrating leadership, must counter this test monovision.

The analysis of data is a critical component of examining your work and improving your school. In this chapter, we will explain how schools create a performance dashboard, or a collection of indicators, which function as *meaningful* and *multiple* measures of progress. In addition, we will guide you through the actual analyses of data and provide five specific strategies to engage others in this step. Finally, we will encourage all who are embarking on this step of data analysis to suspend judgment and speculation. For example, it is best to put aside questions such as "What went wrong?" and "Which activity would serve as a quick fix for the problem?" These questions will be answered in later steps.

The Performance Dashboard

As you think about a high-performing school, what are other indicators of success, besides an achievement test? For example, student participation in extra- or cocurricular activities, volunteer hours donated to a school, and teachers' satisfaction levels with administrative support provide valuable data about a school's academic performance and social health. One aspect of analyzing data is to select important and meaningful data to analyze. Although state or local agencies have defined these success indicators typically in a narrow way, we believe there is great value in educators' collectively determining *the school's* additional measures of success, which may expand upon these externally established indicators. We call the collection of key measures or indicators of a school's success the *performance dashboard*.

Much like the indicator panel on a car (e.g., miles, speed, fuel level), the school's performance dashboard consists of several different measures that serve to provide information to the users about the need to slow down, speed up, or add more fuel. Even though your state may require you to provide an annual performance summary to the community, these reports tend to be narrow in scope and focused on results from one test. Using only one or a few performance indicators is like selecting a new car with only one criterion in mind: the one with the highest fuel efficiency. Although fuel efficiency is an important indicator in these times of fluctuating gas prices, selecting a car based *only* on fuel efficiency typically is not how many people purchase cars. New car buyers often consider a variety of features, such as safety ratings, price, color, speed, or body style (and of course, the cup holders).

The key in selecting *performance indicators* for your school is to choose indicators that have meaning and value for the members of a school community. What are some indicators that most of your staff, students, or community would agree are important? If you are not sure, survey your community by asking questions such as "What do you value most in a school?" or "Think about a great school. What would you see?" By selecting a variety of meaningful (emphasis on *meaningful*) indicators and using them to chart progress, a school community can move from school improvement rhetoric to authentic action.

A school could select many performance indicators. To do so, consider what would be additional markers of success for your school. Think about the areas of your school that directly or indirectly relate to student success, such as teacher characteristics, student discipline issues, or parental involvement. You will discover ideas as you reflect on what is important to you. Moreover, if your school has determined its values or beliefs in the form of a vision, mission, or a profile of a graduate, examine these outcome statements for ideas of performance indicators. Over time, your school will select and possibly even create its own set of key measurements to include on the performance dashboard.

To illustrate, student discipline records and office referrals can be used to develop performance indicators, as student behavior is a result of many components, including the social climate of your school, the adults' expectations, the students' expectations, the levels of trust, the quality of teaching, and the students' motivation and engagement, to name a few. Typically, a good performance indicator is one that stimulates analysis and can result in a number of interpretations. In the example of student behavior, a school might select one of several indicators, such as the number of referrals, the number of suspensions, or the number of fights. Indicators on the dashboard serve as marking points; if referrals have doubled in the past year, the indicator (number of referrals) provides a starting place and a comparison point or benchmark for future analysis. The performance indicator can serve only as a marker; further questioning is needed to explore possible causes and potential solutions. Exploring these types of questions will be described in the Framework in Steps 3, 4, and 5.

Tool 2.1 provides additional ideas to help you consider what might be essential measures of success for your school. You can use this list and the suggestions provided in this section with your school team to select key indicators for the performance dashboard. Take caution to keep the indicators to a manageable number by starting small and adding more over time. Some of the data might not be readily available, and processes may need to be changed in order to collect the desired data. When possible, it is practical to consider existing data and resources available for collection and analysis. What information does your school collect now? What reports are you or your secretary required to submit? What information is already stored in electronic databases?

Identifying key performance indicators with the input of your teachers (and possibly students or the community) is one way to build a collective spirit of improvement in your school. In addition to the key performance indicators on the school's dashboard, there will be other analyses to consider,

Tool 2.1 Ideas for Performance Indicators and the Performance Dashboard

Use this list as a guide to select possible indicators that would be useful in monitoring the progress and performance of your organization (performance dashboard). Some suggestions are:

1. Limit the number of indicators by starting with a few and adding more over time.

2. Consider the ease of data accessibility when selecting indicators.

3. Involve others in selecting performance indicators.

Performance Indicators About Students

Annual dropout rate
Percentage of students graduating on time
Students exceeding the graduation requirements
Students with 95% of higher passing rates on examinations
Number of students taking college entrance examinations
Student attendance rates
Average score on college entrance examinations (SAT, ACT)
Percentage of students participating in extracurricular activities
Number of community service hours worked by students
Percentage of students attending tutorials
Course passing rates
Percentage of students earning state recognition in fine arts activities
Student representation by ethnicity in special education and advanced programs
Percentage of girls enrolled in advanced science and math courses

Performance Indicators About Staff

Percentage of completed career counseling appointments with students
Teacher turnover rates
Percentage of students/staff who demonstrate proficiency in technology
Number of professional development hours/training completed
Staff attendance rates
Satisfaction levels with school

Other Performance Indicators

Percentage of parents who attended teacher-parent conferences
Number of volunteer hours donated to the school
Number of books read or accessed

depending on the programs and situations in the school. So, the performance dashboard does not limit you to only these indicators but instead serves as your school's vital signs for improvement. Defining your own measures of success is empowering and can somewhat liberate you and your teachers from test-score insanity. Having multiple measures can help you expand the definition of success and communicate your school's performance in a way that offers a more accurate and well-rounded checkpoint of your school's success. In the following sections, we will describe the process of data analysis and provide specific examples of how to lead such analyses.

Analyzing Data

What does it mean to analyze data? It means to search for patterns by comparing and combining data that typically are represented by numbers or words. Educators have many daily opportunities to analyze data as they work with students, plan lessons, and monitor progress. What is different about the analysis we are describing in this chapter is that it is focused on improvement, it is systematic rather than random, and it is conducted with a collective group within the school. Perhaps because of time, teachers often do not take part in the analyses of data regarding the school as a whole. Typically, administrators at the district level or campus level analyze school level information, draw conclusions, and then tell the teachers the results, sometimes even outlining the specific solutions. Although it takes time and even training to involve the staff in data analysis, group analysis is probably one of the most important actions a school administrator can take toward creating a culture of improvement.

Finding Time

Finding the time for groups to meet, to analyze data, and to plan solutions can be challenging in schools. One way to find time is to set aside portions at already scheduled meetings such as general faculty meetings, back-to-school meetings, or staff development days. The National Staff Development Council clearly endorses involvement in an improvement process as one of five modes of staff development (Sparks & Loucks-Horsley, 1989). Having experienced this type of staff development, we have found that these days were some of the most productive (and exhausting) for faculty.

Five Steps—Facilitating Data Analysis With Staff

Besides the concepts of scheduling time and analyzing data as a group, school leaders might be uncertain as to ways to orchestrate analyses with groups of people. To help leaders understand analysis, we offer a 5-step process. These steps include the following actions:

- Prepare

- Focus

- Understand

- Observe

- Interpret

Before large groups undertake analyses, attention should be given to *preparation* or organizing data in a useable format. During the *focus* step, the leader provides the necessary background and context of the data being studied as well as reasons why analyses of these specific data are important. In the *understand* step, specific strategies are offered to help teachers interact with and internalize the data, similar to the discovery method common in many classrooms. For the *observe* step, conclusions are offered to summarize the data analysis. Finally, teachers *interpret* the conclusions with general statements. One common practice often omitted when analyzing data is speculating *why* the results are what they are. Making educated guesses as to what caused the results being examined and suggesting possible solutions occur later in the process of examining the work. Applications of these steps with data will be described in future sections.

Preparing for Data Analyses

To prepare for a group meeting where data analyses will be conducted, the leader, facilitator, or a small group (such as the Campus Improvement Team) will select and prepare data sources to analyze. Given that most test results can fill several 3-inch notebook binders, decisions to limit the amount of data will be helpful for the team just beginning this process. For example, selecting student achievement data for the general population of students and for demographic groups can be a logical starting place. It is important that the leader, facilitator, and small group understand the technical terms used in score reports. This information typically is presented in separate documents such as technical reports or glossaries of terms.

Understand Measurement Concepts

Equally important is the need to understand the summary scores (descriptive statistics) used such as percentiles, growth indexes, and scale scores. Understanding these key terms and summary scores will help with interpretation, conclusions, and resulting decisions. On the other hand, a lack of comprehension of these topics can lead to faulty reasoning and misguided actions. A quick lesson or annual review may be helpful in preparing teachers, administrators, and counselors in interpreting scores and sharing results with parents.

A Preparation Check-List. To begin the process of data analysis, the following suggestions are offered:

◆ Gather reports of summary scores of student achievement data for the school, for subject areas, and for grade levels. Include reports that separate groups of students such as those sorted by ethnicity, gender, and economic status.

◆ If the testing instrument has remained consistent, collect reports for the past 3 to 5 years. Longitudinal data are helpful in determining trends in achievement and for analyzing performance over time.

◆ Review other types of data that were collected in the past year by the school, the district, or by groups of teachers. Examples might be parent or student questionnaires, school climate surveys, teacher surveys, or self-assessment scales. If the instrument yields an overall score or subscale scores, take time to understand how to interpret the measure. If the instrument does not yield summary scores, select items on the instrument that will be useful in determining successes, needs, and concerns.

◆ After selecting a few of these data, organize them into reader-friendly formats. Data can be summarized and displayed in charts, graphs, and tables. If an outside vendor has already prepared such graphs and summaries, review to ensure that they are easy to understand.

◆ After these data are prepared, the leader will schedule meetings with faculty to examine the question, "How are we doing?" using the following actions: Focus, Understand, Observe, and Interpret.

Leadership Implications

Data analyses meetings, practiced regularly, can become part of a school's norms or way of doing business. Moreover, these meetings can have multiple purposes. First, the meetings communicate the leader's belief that improvement is important and worth the time. Second, the staff learns and applies a system to reach sound conclusions. Third, staff and community members participate in work that has the potential of building community and consensus, which are characteristic of high-performing schools. However, these data analyses meetings require thought and preparation to be successful. These steps, such as developing an agenda, gathering the materials, and planning the process that will be used to guide the staff though the analyses, will result in meetings that faculty and staff believe are meaningful rather than examples of wasted time. Moreover, a well-planned and well-executed first meeting can positively influence future attitudes about the value of data analysis. In summary, it is important to select a few data sources to begin the process of data analysis and to prepare the data in visuals such as charts, tables, and graphs that can be presented to faculty. All of these actions are important in the preparation for data analysis.

Examples and Applications of Analyzing Data

To illustrate the data analysis process, three indicators for one middle school will be reviewed in the following examples. The improvement team at ABC Middle School selected 15 measures to serve as indicators for its performance dashboard. Following are some examples of these measures and the analyses conducted by the staff. Examples given are teacher turnover rates, Grade 7 mathematics examination scores, and ethnic representation among students receiving special education services.

Example 1 of Analyzing Data: Teacher Turnover Rates

Although some attrition occurs due to relocations, pregnancies, and retirement, high teacher turnover can be particularly problematic for school teams committed to improvement. School administrators may struggle to find qualified replacements during summer vacation; existing teachers must retrain and support newly hired team members. Aside from the need for additional resources to support new faculty, high teacher turnover rates can

Table 2.1

ABC Middle School Teacher Turnover Rates for 3 years

	Teachers beginning the school year	Same teachers returning the following school year	Teacher turnover rate	State average turnover rate
Year 3	60	53	11.66%	14.6%
Year 2	55	46	16.40%	13.9%
Year 1	50	39	22.00%	14.1%

signal potential problems in many areas of the school. Teacher turnover rates have been indicators of particular interest for ABC Middle School. Presented next will be a step-by-step description of how the principal used five strategies for data analysis (prepare, focus, understand, observe, interpret) to analyze the data with the staff.

Following is an explanation of the five strategies of analysis.

1. **Prepare.** To prepare, the principal worked with the school secretary to gather and create the information shown in Table 2.1. Next, the principal set aside 20 minutes at a monthly faculty meeting to lead data analyses activities (Step 2 in the Framework) for this indicator, teacher turnover.

2. **Focus.** During the meeting, the principal modeled the data analyses strategies (focus, understand, observe, and interpret). To provide focus, teachers were given pens and highlighters and asked to search for key words in the table heading, columns, and rows to understand what the numbers represented. Such interaction with the numbers is a strategy that can bring focus to data analysis. In this case, teacher turnover rate, or more specifically the percentage of teachers who did not return the following school year, is what is represented in Table 2.1. It is important to allow time for reflecting and asking questions about what the data mean. Allow the participants to talk about the meanings rather than quickly explaining the findings to them, as this allows the participants an opportunity to connect with data.

3. **Understand.** To help with understanding patterns presented in the data, teachers were asked to tally the percent of change from one year to the next. Plus (+) and minus (–) signs were placed to indicate increases

Table 2.2

Demonstration of Marking System for Analysis of Table 2.1

	Teachers beginning the school year	Same teachers returning the following school year	Teacher turnover rate	State average turnover rate
Year 3	60	53	11.66% (−4.74%)	14.6% (+0.7%)
Year 2	55	46	16.40% (−5.6%)	13.9% (−0.2)
Year 1	50	39	22.00%	14.1%

or decreases, along with the difference of change. With teacher turnover rates, lower numbers indicate that more teachers return to the school, so in this case, minus signs (–) indicate progress. Although one person could have prepared this type of marking in advance, by having each teacher mark his/her own copy of the results, the principal increased engagement and interest of all the staff members. An example of using the marking system is shown in the third and fourth column in Table 2.2

4. **Observe.** After the staff marked the charts, the principal asked and wrote a question to guide this stage of the review: "Considering only the data presented, what did you observe?" Responses to this question included:

◆ "We are below the state average."

◆ "Our turnover rate has decreased each year while our teacher allotments have increased. "

◆ "Our turnover rate has decreased about 10% in the past 3 years."

On occasion, a teacher stated a possible reason for these changes such as retirements or better benefits in other schools. The principal acknowledged such responses without allowing a debate to ensue, bringing focus back to the question—what do these data say? School administrators and teachers, being the skilled problem solvers that they are, may have impatience with focusing only on the data reported. However, the causal statements should be addressed in future steps. One idea is to record these thoughts on a separate chart "Thoughts for Later." This strategy of capturing ideas for the future saves time and validates responses while keeping the focus on analyzing data rather than exploring root causes. In this step, Analyzing the Data, the focus should remain on the data presented.

5. **Interpret.** The final stage in the 5-step process involves interpreting the data. What conclusions can be drawn from the evidence? Reviewing the observations, the principal might ask, "What do these observations mean?" One example of an interpretation is that ABC Middle School is experiencing a degree of success with retaining many of its teachers. In Step 3, Developing Deeper Understanding, more information will be explored to determine possible reasons so that this success can continue.

Example 2 of Analyzing Data: Grade 7 Mathematics Performance

A second example of analyzing data involves the use of results from the school's annual state performance examinations. As typical in many states, the annual state examinations measure each student's understanding of the state curricula objectives. Although you may have analyzed test score performance many times, we offer suggestions for involving your staff in this analysis and apply the five strategies for analysis. Because the principal decided to conduct multiple analyses of the school's performance on state examinations, he designated a half day of staff development time to this review. Following is an explanation of the five strategies of analysis.

1. **Prepare.** To prepare, the principal divided the ABC Middle School staff into teams to analyze subject area and grade-level achievement. The state agency provided the school with summary reports, and these were copied and distributed to each staff member. The following example in Table 2.3 highlights the Grade 7 mathematics passing rates.

2. **Focus.** To focus the activity, the principal explained the importance of student mastery of skills. Next the principal balanced the presentation with a discussion of the limitations of using one test given on one day to determine student achievement levels.

3. **Understand**. Using the same strategy explained in the previous example, staff members discussed that the percentages represented the proportion of students meeting the minimum standard. In this case, the minimum standard score was established at 70%. Clarification of this concept helped the teachers understand what the numbers represented and what they did not. For example, the percentages in Tables 2.3 and 2.4 do not indicate students' average actual scores on

Table 2.3

Grade 7 Mathematics Examination, Average Percent of Students Meeting the Standard

	ABC Middle School	Comparison group of similar schools	District	State
Year 3	76%	88%	87%	80%
Year 2	82%	87%	81%	77%
Year 1	81%	85%	80%	74%

the exams, rather only the proportion of students who scored at least a 70% or higher on the exam. Next, teachers tallied the percent of change for each year.

Now, we invite you to experience the analysis process. Grab a pencil and mark the data in Table 2.3 with plusses (+) and minuses (–). Follow by reviewing the data and noting changes and patterns. Then, answer the question, "What do you observe?"

4. **Observe**. Following are some of the possible observations from data in Table 2.3:

 ◆ The school's Grade 7 math examination passing rates are lower in Year 3 whereas the state, the district, and comparison schools' passing rates have increased over the past 3 years.

 ◆ The school's passing rates have remained lower than the comparison schools.

 ◆ The school's seventh graders had higher passing rates than did students in the district or the state in Year 1 and 2, but not in Year 3.

 ◆ Almost one-fourth of the seventh graders did not meet the math standard passing score in Year 3.

5. **Interpret**. After various observations were recorded, the staff considered the question, "What does this mean?" Many teachers concluded that student performance in Grade 7 math was a concern and that the students could reach higher levels of performance on this test. Not discussed in this step were possible reasons why student performance was lower than expected. Comments about possible causes were recorded and saved for further discussions as outlined in Chapter 3.

Example 3 of Analyzing Data: Grade 7 Mathematics Demographic Groups

Continuing in the same format, the team continued to analyze the performance of demographic groups in the school. The more common demographic groups are shown in Table 2.4; however, other groups could be formed such as students in advanced courses, students new to the school, and students with continuous enrollment in the school for the past 3 years. Following is an explanation of the five strategies of analysis.

1. **Prepare**. The principal distributed copies of Table 2.4 to the staff members.

2. **Focus**. When analyzing demographic group performance, the principal or facilitator might explain that in an effective school, small or insignificant discrepancies will exist among the various groups. This philosophy is grounded in principles of equity and opportunity for all students, regardless of ethnicity, gender, or disadvantage. Such results have been documented with teachers who collectively use improvement processes and analyses tools, similar to those shared in this book, to improve the learning and teaching in their schools. Much information about effective schools results from website searches and book reviews.

3. **Understand**. Using numbers to rank the various groups, each teacher compared results across the rows. For example, in all 3 years, girls scored higher than boys did, so teachers marked girls with "1" and boys with a "2" for each of the years. Continuing with the remaining demographic groups, teachers marked "White" with a "1" for each year. This simple system helps to organize the results for further

Table 2.4

Grade 7 Mathematics Examination, Percent of Students Meeting Standards, Demographic Groups

	School	Boys	Girls	African American	Hispanic	White	Eco Dis*	LEP**
Year 3	76%	72%	79%	67%	65%	82%	61%	36%
Year 2	82%	79%	84%	74%	75%	80%	70%	40%
Year 1	81%	77%	83%	65%	75%	80%	66%	41%

* students with an economic disadvantage   ** students with Limited English Proficiency

observations. Next, working in each column, teachers used "+" and "−" to mark increases and decreases from Year 1 to Year 2 and Year 2 to Year 3. In this example, data were analyzed across groups (vertical analysis) and among years (horizontal analysis).

4. **Observe**. Once teachers have analyzed the passing rates in Table 2.4, some of their possible responses to the question, "What do you observe?" are as follows:

   ◆ More seventh-grade girls met the minimum standard in math than seventh-grade boys did for each of the 3 years, ranging from differences of 3% to 6%.

   ◆ All demographic groups' passing rates were lower in Year 3 as compared to Year 1 except for African American and White students.

   ◆ African American and Hispanic students' passing rates were lower by about 15% compared to White students.

   ◆ Of all the demographic groups, the LEP students had the lowest passing rates, with less than two fifths of the students meeting the standard.

   ◆ In Year 2, more students met the minimum standards in all demographic groups (except for Whites) than the groups did in Year 3.

   ◆ About 6% fewer students met the standard in Year 3 than they did in Year 2.

5. **Interpret (with Caution!)** To draw a general conclusion, ask, "What does this mean?" In regards to the performance of demographic groups, one misinterpretation by some well-intentioned principals and teachers has been to target specific groups of students for interventions based on the group characteristic. Remember, in this stage of analysis, the focus is on finding patterns in large groups. In later steps, deeper explorations will yield questions that are more pointed and answers that are more specific. An example showing the incorrect use of demographic group data occurred in one school where the economically disadvantaged group passing rates were about 20% lower than those were of other groups. As a result, each grade level planned activities specifically for the students in this group. In the example in Table 2.4, 36% of the students in the economically disadvantaged group more than likely would not need this intervention; therefore, it could be seen as discriminatory to include all students of a demographic group to receive an intervention. More appropriate would be to consider individual student scores, thereby designing

interventions for individual students and then forming small instructional groups organized by various intervention strategies, not by grouping characteristics.

Example 4 of Analyzing Data: Ethnic Distribution of Students Receiving Special Education Services

Continuing with the data analyses of key performance indicators, ABC Middle School focused on its students receiving special education services. Special education programs have remained a topic of interest, and in recent years the issue of disproportionate representation of students receiving such services has been highlighted. Specifically, The Individuals with Disabilities Education Act, Part B (IDEA-Part B) requires both states and their local school districts to report and remedy the disproportionate representation of racial and ethnic groups in special education. For more information about this topic, conduct a web search on the Internet using the search term *significant disproportionality*. Following is an explanation of the five strategies of analysis.

1. **Prepare**. To prepare the data in Table 2.5, the principal consulted the director of special services for the campus information and accessed two additional websites to retrieve the state information.

2. **Focus**. With the staff, using the initial analyses techniques, the principal focused attention on the meaning of the indicators reported in Table 2.5. The table shows the percent of students in the school by

Table 2.5

Ethnic Distribution of All Students and Students Receiving Special Education Services

	Total School	School Special Education (9.5%)	Total State	State Special Education (10%)
African American	15.3%	22.8%	14.4%	18.78%
Hispanic	29.8%	40.1%	46.3%	42.15%
White	46.9%	35.2%	35.7%	37.3%
Native American	0.3%	0.9%	0.3%	0.43%
Other	7.7%	1.0%	3.3%	1.34%

ethnicity and the percent of students in special education by ethnicity. The same data are reported for the state and these can be compared with the school's ratios.

3. **Understand.** Next, the staff marked differences for each ethnic group, working across each row, comparing the proportion of African American students in the school to these students' membership in special education programs and comparing the special education rates of the school to those of the state.

4. **Observe.** After considering the question, "What do you observe?" the following statements were generated:

   ♦ African American, Hispanic, and Native Americans were overrepresented and Whites were underrepresented in special education.

   ♦ The largest gap for the school occurs with Hispanics who are overrepresented by about 10%. Next were African Americans who are overrepresented in special education by 7.5%

   ♦ The school's overall rate of students in special education (9.5%) was lower than the state (10%).

   ♦ For the state, overrepresentation occurred for African Americans and Whites but not for Hispanics.

5. **Interpret.** Asking, "What does this mean?," teachers concluded that although their special education rates were lower than those of the state, ethnic distributions in special education were unbalanced in their school.

Summing Up

In this chapter, we explained the concept of the performance dashboard and encouraged you to consider the measures that would be most meaningful in determining progress in the various target areas. For those leaders and staff members who struggle with where or how to start, we suggested a few practical strategies to organize data and involve staff in analyses. In addition, a 5-step data analysis process was shared as a tool to guide faculty (prepare, focus, understand, observe, and interpret). As you and your staff continue to analyze data, you may determine different ways to summarize and display data and you will continue to discover new data sources.

If you were already familiar with the processes described in this chapter, first consider the extent to which your staff is involved in the analysis process. What are the possibilities for including students, parents, and other campus supporters in the process? Second, consider the extent to which data analysis has become a part of your culture or "the way we do things around here." You can strengthen the focus of analysis by leading monthly analysis activities, such as regularly presenting a summary of some data and working through the steps described in this chapter. Starting with a few examples, planning for weekly or monthly reviews, and limiting the sessions to 20 minutes will help to build a consistent practice and to minimize negative experiences with analysis.

Finally, try to contain judgment and avoid speculation in the process of analyzing data. After reaching some conclusions, it is natural to wonder why something may have occurred. Unfortunately, we have observed that some leaders and teachers point fingers quickly, often toward other people! Have you heard "It was the new, inexperienced teachers," or "Last year's teachers did not teach the concepts"? Although you may discover some truth in these statements later in the process, by allowing such conversations to exist in the same space as analysis, you essentially shut down open and honest problem solving for the future. Trust will be negatively affected, as individuals will observe that it is not "safe" to share weaknesses. Even if some teachers are not being blamed, they may predict that blame is coming and take on a defensive stance. If you notice that blame is part of your culture, we recommend that you review Setting the Foundation essentials in Chapter 1 and seek additional resources to help rebuild trust. Such essentials are foundational for genuine analysis and further progress.

> **Remember:**
> Analyzing data is both a skill and an ongoing process used by teams to examine and improve their work.

Reflection Questions:

1. When you receive the campus test score reports, do you prefer time to digest the results yourself or do you involve staff immediately in this initial analysis?

2. To what extent do you understand the technical aspects of the test reports you receive, such as what the terms mean, what the tests measure, and what the summary scores represent (e.g., means, standard deviations, stanines, percentiles)?

3. How competent is your staff in the skill of data analysis?

4. To what extent is analysis a part of your school culture?

5. How do individuals at your campus perceive analysis and its importance in improving your work?

Examining the Work: Developing Deeper Understanding

And now you know . . . the rest of the story.

Paul Harvey, radio broadcaster

Knowing is not understanding. There is a great difference between knowing and understanding: You can know a lot about something and not really understand it.

Charles Kettering, Inventor

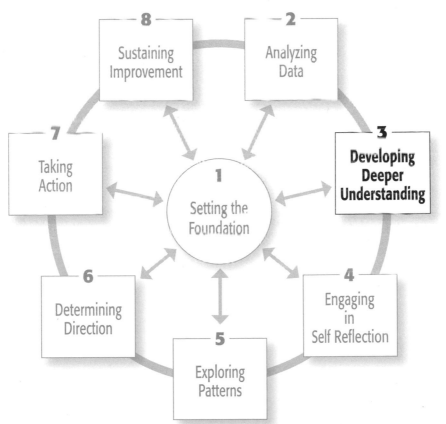

Data are essential in understanding the work in schools and identifying the outcomes. However, data do not provide all the answers. In fact, an over-reliance on numbers can be just as harmful as failing to use data in the first place. In almost every situation, gaps in information remain, and these gaps might be critical to understanding the complete situation and making informed decisions. For example, perhaps a school's performance on the annual math examination was lower this year compared with previous years. The numbers can be used to reveal that the scores dropped and can be used to identify the most problematic skill areas. However, what the numbers do not and cannot reveal is *why* the scores dropped or how one should specifically proceed with helping students be successful. The test scores by themselves can never tell *why* things are happening. To develop this deeper level of understanding, more information is needed, and the leader must use other types of approaches to gather more and different kinds of data.

Education is a people-centered business, and people tend to be complicated. To understand what a person does and why, the leader has to know and understand things that are personal to that individual. Often, situations are not what they appear on the surface, and at face value one usually lacks the background information and relevant details to make informed decisions and choices. In order to understand people, knowing their story is important. Thus, a major part of developing deeper understanding is to ask, "What are the stories related to this person, situation, or school?"

In this chapter, specific strategies for developing deeper understanding are discussed in depth. These include the following: (a) active listening (listen *to* the story *for* the story), (b) interviewing (collecting information from individuals; using effective techniques; building rapport; acquiring authentic data), (c) observing (both formally and informally), and (d) conducting focus groups (collecting information in a group setting). Attention is also given to helping leaders understand the importance of politics and the media and noting how people's personal, political, or professional agendas might affect their decisions and actions.

Techniques for Developing Understanding

Many of the techniques for developing deeper understanding could be classified as qualitative research techniques, such as interviews, focus groups, observations, and open-ended questionnaires or surveys. Qualitative data collection and analyses allow one to describe, to give meaning, and to explore phenomena that cannot be expressed adequately through quantitative data. Numbers, even statistics, do not tell the whole story. Qualitative techniques allow one to gather data that will help fill in the gaps left by numerical data. In essence, these types of data are ideal for developing deeper understanding. Qualitative inquiry facilitates the understanding of people, places, and things. Generally, qualitative techniques allow for inductive processes where one takes a multitude of data, sorts through it to locate patterns, and proposes meanings to develop conclusions and understanding.

Just as quantitative data have their limitations, so do qualitative data. For example, purely qualitative techniques can be very time consuming. Interviewing teachers, conducting focus groups, and observing behaviors all take time, which can be a very scarce resource for school leaders. Qualitative approaches also do not allow conclusions to be generalized to other settings, meaning that what is found for one department, group of students, or campus will not necessarily apply to another group. In addition, these sorts of techniques cannot be used to establish cause and effect relationships.

With these limitations in mind, mixed method approaches, which combine both numbers and words, are ideal for developing understanding. Take, for example, teacher evaluations. The quantitative aspect of teacher evaluations involves such questions as, What are the grade distributions for the teacher's classes? How many discipline referrals has the teacher written? How many parent complaints have been registered for this teacher? These questions might give information for the basis of an evaluation. However, a much more accurate and effective evaluation can be developed if the leader develops a deeper understanding of these questions and what is occurring in the teacher's classroom. Some techniques to gather this information would include observations in the teacher's classroom and interactions with the students. Individual meetings with the teacher may reveal the context and challenges present in the classroom. In addition, a review of the teacher's lesson plans or written communication with parents might be useful. These techniques allow the leader to produce a more accurate evaluation and provide information to help the teacher plan for further improvement.

Quantitative findings help identify the "what" but not the "why." On the other hand, qualitative techniques help understand "why" and "how" situations are happening—they provide a broader understanding of some of the different factors that affect a particular area. For example, when considering low test scores or an increase in high school dropouts, the numbers alone will not help to resolve the issue. Although being aware of the numbers and ensuring the accuracy of those data is important, it is important to realize that low test scores and dropouts are both caused and affected by a myriad of complex factors. These factors are typically unique to a particular setting, context, community, or even individual. Thus, a one-size-fits-all approach rarely works in education. Critical in developing deeper understanding is to answer questions such as the following: What is the situation at hand? Why might this be happening? What are the stories of the people involved? How do we take this information and move forward?

Example—Application of Developing Deeper Understanding

In Chapter 2, Table 2.5, we provided data about the ethnic distribution of students receiving special education services. One observation was that African American and Hispanic students were represented in special education at higher rates than those occurring at state levels. To develop a deeper understanding of this problem, the leader and a group of individuals could brainstorm possibilities and ask more questions. One way to achieve a deeper understanding is to review individual student records to determine when students were admitted, their qualifying disabilities, and their progress towards their individual education plan (IEP) goals and objectives. Another data collection technique would be to observe the students in their classrooms, determine the appropriateness of students' placements, and check for issues of misidentification. In addition, the counselor and teachers of special education could be interviewed for their insights into the problem of over-identification. These various techniques can be helpful in understanding the information presented in Table 2.5.

In addition to collecting additional data at the campus level, leaders should explore information beyond their schools. For example, the leader might ask for information to determine the campuses where students in special education were first identified. Further, the district's administrators for special education might provide insight regarding the system as a whole. Some questions might be, In what grades were they referred and by whom? Is there a pattern where students were identified in a certain grade, or perhaps on a certain campus? The administrators for special education can discuss the patterns within the program, relevant policies and procedures, or other important considerations at the district level that might be affecting the situation. By including district administrators, the leader can determine if the pattern of over-identification is part of a systemic issue and/ or a practice unique to a campus or for a group of students. Next, visits with district special education teachers may provide additional perspective as to why certain students are over-identified. In addition, the leader may have to involve other district-level departments (such as the special education department), as the identification of students for special programs also has to be addressed to administrators beyond the campus level.

Gaining a deeper understanding allows a leader to recognize what the problem is and where it needs to be addressed, including when it should be addressed at an organizational level beyond the campus. This sort of understanding emphasizes the fact that a school is an open system, where units must interact and depend on each other, because they also influence each other; schools are not a closed system where any one entity operates in isolation or in a vacuum. This further demonstrates why it is important for school leaders to have a good working relationship with groups outside of their immediate campus personnel, such as the special education office and others. Deeper understanding in most situations involves concern for individuals as well as for the system as a whole. In other words, one is looking at data from a viewpoint of multiple perspectives. How does a given situation impact students? Teachers? Parents? The community? The school as a whole? In developing deeper understanding, leaders are responsible for maintaining a multi-perspective understanding of how a situation or decision affects a variety of groups. We have provided Tool 3.1 to help you select appropriate data collection techniques that will facilitate deeper understanding.

Technique: Active Listening

A critical component of developing deeper understanding is the ability to listen actively. In fact, active listening is one of the best skills that a leader can develop, for it serves one well in so many ways such as conflict resolution, developing understanding, and even just keeping out of trouble! With active listening, you must make sure that you are attentive to the speaker and that you really understand and comprehend what is being said. Can you reflect and repeat the essence of what you heard? If not, then you should ask questions that will lead to greater clarity. To be a good listener, one needs to avoid interrupting or finishing the other person's sentences. It is also important to avoid reflecting the conversation toward yourself, such as the following replies: "*I* remember when that happened to *me* . . . " or "*I* know exactly how you feel." The activity presented in Tool 3.2 can be used to help you practice active listening with your staff. You can use this tool with teachers to improve listening and observation skills, which will help in the overall development of deeper understanding.

Tool 3.1 Selecting Data Collection Techniques

Data Source	Advantages	Disadvantages
Interviews	Provides rich data Opportunity to probe further	Time-consuming Requires cooperation of participants Requires interviewing skills
Observations	Provides contextual viewpoint	Behavior may change because of observer's presence
Focus Groups	Multiple perspectives Obtain a large amount of data	Can encourage "group-think" Some individuals might be hesitant to share their feelings in a group
Documents	Easy to access	Information may be incomplete or inaccurate
Questionnaires	Quick source of data Can reach more people	Limited follow-up Offers less depth

Based on the advantages and disadvantages identified, which type(s) of data might be most informative?

Tool 3.2 Practicing the Art of Active Listening

Working with a group of three—one is the speaker, one is the listener, and one is the observer, individuals will practice their listening skills. Each person in the group will take turns with each of the three roles. Each conversation should last about 5 minutes.

◆ The Speaker should talk about an issue that is important to him/her, such as something happening at work, with the family, or with a friend. (The subject is not important and should not distract from the activity.)

◆ The Listener will practice active listening skills, making sure not to project his/her own feelings or opinions into the situation. The Listener should ask clarifying questions and paraphrase what is heard, allowing the Speaker to affirm or correct his/her thoughts.

◆ The Observer will watch the interaction between the Speaker and Listener and describe the listening attempts and nonverbal behaviors.

◆ When the Speaker is finished talking or when time is called, each person will reflect on the conversation and the listening behaviors. The Observer will describe the Listener's behaviors and the Speaker's responses. The Listener will reflect on his/her listening and the Speaker will discuss ways that the Listener was helpful.

Technique: Interviews

There are varieties of strategies that you can use to search for deeper understanding and make meaning out of data. One way to do this is through an interview. Interviews can involve a wide array of people, such as central office personnel, faculty or staff from feeder schools, and of course constituencies from your own campus, such as teachers, staff, parents, other administrators, or even students (with parent permission). Interviews quite simply involve a question and answer process between the interviewer and a single participant. Interviews can be structured, with a purposefully pre-developed set of questions, or unstructured, where questions are spontaneous and vary by person and topic. When developing interview questions, be sure that they align with the problem and purpose of what it is you want to know. Great questions are not so great if they do not give you useful information. Questions should be open-ended and allow for maximum opportunities for participants to respond. Each question should ask or focus on only one topic so that each important concept is addressed individually. You should be careful to avoid leading questions that might convince or suggest to someone that you are looking for a particular type of response. Likewise, it is important, especially as a campus leader, to avoid showing any type of bias during an interview. Do not forget that body language, facial expressions, tone of voice, and other non-verbal cues of those being interviewed are excellent sources of additional information.

Technique: Document Analysis

Documents can vary from personal to legal records that exist in schools. Some documents might be organizational in nature; these can be internal documents, such as those shared within a department, or external documents that an organization distributes to the public. Organizational documents might include employee memos, flyers, or salary records. Electronic documents, which could include emails, blogs, or text messages, are documents that should also be considered. Public records and personnel files can also be sources of important documents that provide key information about a person or situation. These items could include grades, attendance, disciplinary records, employment history, letters of commendation (or reprimand), and other such communications. Although documents alone are rarely sufficient to provide enough data, they are excellent sources of support information in combination with data collected from interviews and observations.

Technique: Questionnaires

Questionnaires typically are considered a tool for gathering quantitative data. Still, they can be useful in developing deeper understanding when they include open-ended questions where participants record their thoughts or perceptions on a given topic. There are disadvantages to using a questionnaire to collect data. For example, with a written questionnaire, you lack the opportunity to probe deeper into participants' responses. When respondents provide short answers, you are unable to ask for clarification or further detail. You are also unable to clarify the questions to the participants—for example, if the questions are not clear, you have no way to explain what is meant to those persons completing the surveys. For the same reason, you must also make sure that your written instructions and purpose of the questionnaire are clear. On a questionnaire, only the written data are available—there are no non-verbal cues, no body language, no facial expressions, no tone of voice, or any other contextual elements that might add to the richness of the information. Thus, we suggest caution in the overuse or exclusive use of collecting information by questionnaires.

Technique: Focus Groups

In essence, a focus group could be considered a group interview and can be useful in combination with individual interviews and surveys. Focus groups can provide data from a larger number of individuals in the same amount of time as compared to individual interviews. Typically, a focus group involves 7-10 persons, plus a facilitator or co-facilitators. The facilitator may or may not be the school leader and should be chosen carefully as the facilitator will likely influence the levels of honest responses provided by participants. Focus groups allow for multiple perspectives and allow participants to share ideas with one another. Thus, the interactions of group members can help or hinder the collection of information. In fact, individuals with strong personalities might dominate a focus group and sometimes their views will influence the ideas of others. Participants might be intimidated to share their honest ideas in front of others, or they may be hesitant to speak in front of those with dominant personalities. The facilitator can help to alleviate some anxiety by explaining who will see the data and how the data will be used. The facilitator should emphasize that there are no right or wrong answers, and that not everyone has to agree with one another. In addition, the facilitator will need to ensure that the group remains respectful of all individuals and that everyone has an opportunity to be heard.

Summing Up

Developing deeper understanding can be as important for learning about the school's strengths as it is for learning about its weaknesses. For example, in one school presented in Chapter 2, teachers continued to return to their positions each year, resulting in a very low teacher turnover rate, which is clearly a strength. Even with positive trends and results, the leader should dig deeper to learn why this trend is taking place. The purpose for developing deeper understanding of the low teacher turnover rates is to identify possible causes for this result and identify actions that can be maintained and continued. By building on these strengths, the leader can use this information to encourage teachers and even share with other campuses and districts. Some ways that the leader could begin a search for deeper understanding of low teacher turnover rates is to brainstorm possible root causes and/or reasons for this positive trend. Some actions might include:

- conducting a survey on climate issues related to the campus

- evaluating changes in external forces that might have taken place, such as a salary increase

- examining levels of mentor support

To learn more, the leader or other appointed individuals can conduct focus groups with new teachers, mentors, department chairs, or even central office personnel. In addition, documents related to recruitment, staff development, and personnel benefits may be helpful as well. In summary, leaders and their teachers who use multiple and varied data collection techniques are more likely to gain deeper understanding.

Remember:
Developing deeper understanding is critical for you to have all the pieces for solving the puzzle of school improvement. Data are just part of the picture—deeper understanding allows you to make meaning of the situation, to understand *why* instead of just *what*.

Reflection Questions:

1. Think of a situation on your campus that requires deeper understanding. Why is this issue important? What do you already know about the situation?

2. What else do you need to know besides "just the facts"?

3. How can you search for further meaning?

4. Can you conduct interviews or focus groups? If so, with whom and why?

5. What will a deeper understanding of the situation allow you to do?

Step 4

Examining the Work: Engaging in Self-Reflection

There is only one thing more painful than learning from experience and that is not learning from experience.

Archibald McLeish, poet, writer, and Librarian of Congress

A professor traveled the same route to her university for 4 years. One day she visited a student teacher who taught at a local middle school. The professor spent the day at the middle school observing. She met her student teacher's students, other teachers, and the administrators. The next day, as she traveled her same route to the university, she noticed a huge billboard sign about that school. In class that week, she said to the student teacher, "I saw the new sign for your school. It's very nice." The student responded, "That sign isn't new, it's been up there for years." Perhaps you have had a similar experience of being unaware of something in your environment. Gary Howard (1999) has written a book about how educators deal with diversity called *You Can't Teach What You Don't Know*. But in truth, perhaps it goes beyond even the warning of Howard's book title. Until the professor knew something about the middle school, she did not even see the sign about the school. One cannot even *see* what one does not know, let alone teach what is unknown! This is why Step 4, Engaging in Self-Reflection, is so important. Reflection allows one to see what is unknown so that one can begin to understand, which ultimately informs change.

Seeing the Changing World More Clearly

Change is fast-paced and dynamic in both our world and schools today. Generational differences are growing and a gap between educators and students is ever widening and complex. In fact, the United States is developing a generation gap between aging White adults and a young, growing minority population. Forty-seven percent of children under age 5 are minorities, as are 43% of young people under age 20. The median age among non-Hispanic Whites has increased to 41.1 while the median age of Hispanics is 27.7. According to Moore and Overberg (2009), the demographic shift is most dramatic among kids under 20. In fact, Mark Mather of the Population Reference Bureau noted, "They [kids under 20] really are the groups that are driving these changes" (Moore & Overberg, 2009, p. 1A). In addition, changes in family structure are occurring. Today, less than one fourth of U.S. households are made up of married couples with children under age 18; single mothers head 7.2% of households; and few children have a caregiver at home who does not work outside the home (Trotter, 2001). Poverty is an increasing concern since nearly 1 in 5 children in the United States live in poverty, and extreme poverty is becoming more concentrated in some inner cities (National Poverty Center, 2008).

Margaret Mead (1966) wrote about the importance of understanding the changing world because "each generation must begin anew and, in doing so, must stand on the shoulders of the one before" (Preface). Such diversity extends from class, ethnicity, race, and age, to language, sexual preference, gender, and learning styles, to name a few.

Before educators can ask the right questions that will lead to equitable teaching and learning environments for this diverse population, they should first see themselves and others clearly. Remember, one cannot even *see* what one does not know. As such, there are three self-reflective questions to consider: Who am I? What biases do I have? Why am I an educator?

Who Am I?

Bingham (2001) wrote of the unique challenge of educators to understand themselves and others by noting the "most important recognitive question: How can human dignity be acknowledged again and again?" (p. 5). This question has educational implications for student identity, which should be addressed by educators. After all, it is the educator who "mirrors back" to the student an "affirming sense" of who he is throughout the school day (Bingham, 2001, p. 34).

Who am I? Valerie Pang (2005) describes culture as "the air we breathe in, it is all around us" (p. 37). Thus, people are all products of our cultures. It is this invisible culture that surrounds us that determines what we value and how we respond to our life experiences. Do we treat others with respect and value their inherent human dignity, or do we stereotype those who are different from us with a limited and sometimes negative view of their experiences? Do we put a hierarchical value on experiences so that middle-class values are more "right" than those of someone from poverty? When we act on these beliefs in this limited way, we lose the opportunity to see our common experiences and to enrich our lives by valuing our differences. How can we determine if children's cultural experiences differ from ours if we do not take time to understand our own culture? Consider your own culture for a moment and answer the questions provided in Tool 4.1. Reflect on your answers because they explain much about who you are, and, ultimately, the kind of inquiry questions that you will ask about your school.

Tool 4.1 Who Am I?

- What are my goals in life?

- What do others expect of me?

- What do I expect of myself?

- What do I value?

- Who has been a great influence in my life?

- How did this individual influence me?

- What motivates me?

- How do I show others that I care about them?

- What were my experiences when I was in school?

- Who do I think is different from me?

- What do I believe about people who are different from me?

- What kind of relationships do I have with others?

- What kind of relationships do I have with others who are different from me?

What Biases Do I Have?

Few people believe that they are biased or that they ever discriminate based on their biases. Yet, the truth is most of us have biases and prejudices. One exercise that you can use for reflection is called *20 Categories*. Write down 20 words that describe you. Obvious categories will be your gender, ethnicity, and age group. Other categories may be your religion, political views, occupation, educational levels, and family status. Continue the exercise until you can list 20 categories or adjectives. Next, consider the following questions: How has my membership in each one of these categories affected my thoughts? My actions? My choice of friends? My exposure to other viewpoints? The life experiences you bring to any situation affect your approach to both the problem and the solution. Although this does not prevent you from being able to make an objective decision, it does reveal areas where you are potentially biased, and an awareness of this bias is critical. Before you can begin to lead a school with a vision of equity for all students, you must do some soul searching and understand what biases you have.

In order to lead others on your campus to be able to examine issues and needs, you must begin with an awareness of your own biases. Take some time and answer the questions in Tool 4.2. Some of the questions are similar to those you answered about who you are in the previous exercise. Now, you might be able to view those questions with a different perspective.

Why Am I an Educator?

From time to time, we, as educators, should examine our purposes for becoming educators and remaining in the role. Elliot Eisner (2006) wrote, "How we teach is ultimately a reflection of why we teach" (p. 44). He then described six "deep satisfactions" that teachers seek from the process of teaching:

1. introducing students to great ideas
2. reaching out to students ensures our own immortality
3. performing and improvising—how something is taught—affects how it is learned
4. creating moments of artistry
5. sharing a passion for education
6. making a difference (p. 45)

Tool 4.2 What Biases Do I Have?

- Do I treat every student (teacher, parent) with the same respect and positive regard?

- In which situations do I stereotype others?

- How often do I stereotype others?

- What do I believe about those who are different from me?

- Do I value characteristics of diverse learners?

- How often do I interact with those who are different from me?

- How does this affect me as an educator?

- How do I react when jokes are told making fun of diverse groups?

- How can I change my actions?

These same six deep satisfactions are not limited to classroom teaching but apply to educational leaders at all levels who serve as role models for students, encourage teachers, and provide leadership for students and teachers.

Many of us became educators with an idealized vision of improving the world by helping students. Too often, we might forget our original mission and passion when we become so busy and challenged by problems. Recently a middle school principal shared the following story:

A ninth-grade boy on the principal's campus was failing all of his classes, he was not attending school regularly, and he was often in trouble with his teachers and peers. The principal and the boy's teachers were all frustrated. One late afternoon, when everyone had gone home and the school was quiet, the principal pulled the boy's file. He read that this young man through the sixth grade had been a model student, made good grades, and never got in trouble. In the summer before he began his seventh-grade year, the boy's parents divorced and the father moved out of state. He had not seen his father in 3 years.

As the principal read the file, he began to see this young man as a "real person" with challenges that were perhaps far greater than the academic problems he was facing at school. The principal said,

"I knew that in order to help this boy academically, we had to help him in the larger scope of his life. I immediately e-mailed his teachers and we set up a meeting for the next day. Our challenge was to help this young man as a person before we could help him as a student."

In other words, the principal realized that no one could TEACH this young man as a student until he could REACH him as a person. Because the principal had self-reflected and knew who he was, understood his own biases, and remembered why he became an educator, he began to see this student through a new lens. Here was a student who needed help—the very reason why the principal had become an educator.

Summing Up

Leaders cannot accurately examine the work to improve schools without following Step 4, Engaging in Self-Reflection. Active self-reflection is a key component in this process. The self-reflective process causes us to see our surroundings with greater awareness. Leaders should spend time rediscovering who they are, identifying their own biases, and remembering their vision for becoming educators (see Tool 4.3). They lead others to do the same and provide time and encouragement to engage in self-reflection at meetings, and in formal and informal discussions. Self-reflection is not a once-a-year activity, but should occur on a continuous basis. Self-reflection is like a magic mirror; as you look into that mirror, you can see yourself reflected from the inside out. Hopefully, what you see is, according to Socrates, the "first key to greatness . . . to be in reality what we appear to be."

> **Remember:**
> It is in seeing that we begin to know. In knowing, we begin to reach for truth. In reaching, we begin to teach and lead.

Reflection Questions:

1. In a six-word sentence, describe who you are.
2. In a six-word sentence, describe what biases you might have.
3. In a six-word sentence, describe what you are doing to understand your biases.
4. In a six-word sentence, describe why you are an educator.
5. What do you believe that educators need to *see* in order to *know*?
6. What do you believe that educators need to *know* in order to *reach*?
7. In reaching others, how will this affect the teaching and leading at your school?
8. How can you incorporate these beliefs into a personal mission statement?

Tool 4.3 Why Am I an Educator?

1. I became an educator because . . .

2. Today I am an educator because . . .

3. This is how my reasons for becoming an educator have changed over time . . .

4. The last time that I felt good about being an educator was . . .

5. My favorite memories as a student have been . . .

6. My favorite memories as a teacher have been . . .

7. My favorite memories as an administrator/leader have been . . .

8. I encourage positive feelings in students and teachers with whom I work when I . . .

9. The lives of today's students are diffcrent from mine in these ways. . .

10. The lives of today's students are the same as mine in these ways . . .

11. In order to renew or sustain my vision for my life as an educator, I need to . . .

Step 5

Examining the Work: Exploring Programmatic Patterns

It is often easier to become outraged by injustice half a world away than by oppression and discrimination half a block from home.

Carl T. Rowan, American journalist

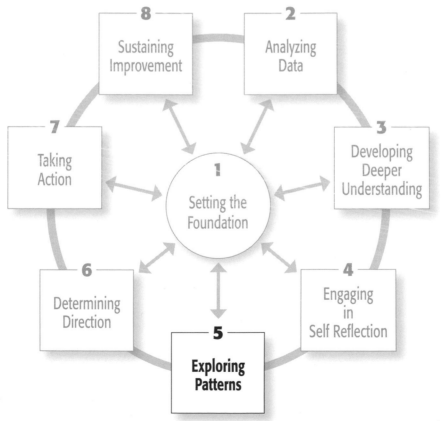

Asking the Right Questions

A few years ago, one of the authors attended a meeting that was focused on issues related to college readiness of high school students. Individuals from the Texas Higher Education Coordinating Board reported that from 2000 to 2004, 188,000 students had enrolled in Texas 4-year colleges and universities. This was the largest increase in Texas history! Indeed, this *was* good news. Further, the goal was that by 2015, 500,000 Texas students would be enrolled in college. It was only 2004, and at this rate, we would enroll 752,000 students by 2015!

However, other questions were asked in regard to these data. For example, how does Texas compare with other states? What are the students' completion rates when following a population of seventh graders through high school? What are the differences among groups, such as those students who are economically disadvantaged? These questions led to the following facts:

◆ When compared with other states, Texas sent a lower percentage of students to higher education than did other states.

◆ When following 255,000 Texas public school seventh graders from 1992, only 82% were still in school in the ninth grade, and only 58% graduated.

◆ Of the 255,000 seventh graders, 45% of these entered higher education, and only 13% of these went on to graduate with a college degree.

◆ Of the students who enrolled in higher education in Texas, economically disadvantaged students of all ethnicities (except Asian) were less likely to enroll.

◆ In regard to the enrollments, target rates were established. The target rates for White students were exceeded by 289.9%, yet only 70.1% of the target was reached for Hispanic students.

Digging deeper revealed that Texas had enrolled more students than ever before. Nevertheless, as more questions were asked and data were analyzed, it was recognized that there was still much improvement needed. If we had only asked the one question—How many students were enrolled in a 4-year college during 2000–2004?—we would have had a false sense of success. Educators who are not sensitive to the achievement gap could look at the reported numbers of new college students and rejoice that the state was already far ahead of projections. But, because we were and are concerned about the different experiences of diverse groups of students, we knew we needed to ask other questions that looked at programmatic experiences of various demographic groups of students. In the process of analysis to action to examine the ongoing processes of school improvement, it was important to consider Step 5 in the Framework for Examining School Improvement, Exploring Programmatic Patterns.

Programmatic Patterns in the Achievement Gap

Examining programmatic patterns is especially useful for investigating the achievement gap. The federal government has been documenting the achievement gap between majority and minority learners since 1969 (Nelson, Palonsky, & McCarthy, 2007). In fact, the central aim of NCLB was to close the achievement gap. Yet, according to Nelson and colleagues, although there have been gains in African American academic achievement, the achievement gap between majority and minority learners continues to widen in some states.

Darling-Hammond (2007) reported that on national assessments in reading, writing, mathematics, and science, Black students' performances lag behind that of White students. In fact, Black students' performances during the 1970s and 1980s, which had been improving, have reversed since 1988, with scores now declining for 13- and 17-year olds since that time. In 2002, the average Black or Hispanic 12th grader read at the same level as the average White eighth-grader (National Center for Education Statistics [NCES], 2005).

The practice of investigating programmatic patterns has shed light on the relationship between poverty and student achievement. For all groups of students except White students, racially segregated schools (which are increasing in the United States) generally have high concentrations of students living in poverty (Orfield, 2001). According to Orfield and Yun (1999), African American students and Hispanic students with limited English speaking proficiencies were more likely to live in urban areas, where schools tended to be overcrowded and had limited resources as compared with suburban school districts with a majority of White students. In fact, Rubinstein-Avila (2006) argued that most school districts were unprepared to handle the population growth of at-risk students.

In Texas for example, the state report card, known as the Academic Excellence Indicator System (AEIS) report published by the Texas Education

Agency (TEA), has shown a performance gap between White students and the students who make up the other groups. The gap is the disparity found by subtracting the minority percentage of passing from the majority percentage of passing a given test ("School Matters," 2006). In Texas, minority students now represent the majority of students but are underperforming compared with their White counterparts. In the 2004-2005 school year, 91% of the White students in Texas passed the reading examination compared with only 77% of the Hispanic students and 76% of African American students. The disparity was even worse in math and science where 84% of White students passed math and 81% passed science while African American students had 57% passing rates in math and 49% in science (TEA, 2005). Of course, what is happening in Texas is just an example, as such programmatic performance patterns exist in other states throughout the nation.

Programmatic Patterns Help to Identify Biases in the School

Programmatic patterns in the school are often a reflection of the biases that exist in the school. Therefore, in order to promote a more just and equitable understanding of educational leadership, today's administrators must have vision for their schools that resonates with practices that reflect a moral obligation to educate all students with respect, compassion, and wisdom. A major challenge to accomplish this is that cultural socialization begins in homes where children are first taught the norms, beliefs, and values of their parents. By the time children come to school, they have already been acculturated into certain behaviors, values, and practices. As educators, it is not for us to de-value a child's culture, yet often this is where much of the conflict begins. Consequently, educators must ask, "What biases are in my school?"

Many of you may remember the textbooks in use when you were in elementary school. It is likely that most pictures of the family included a mother, father, son, daughter, and a dog. Although 30 or 40 years ago this was how families were defined, this family image did not fit everyone's particular cultural experience. For example, a student in one of our classes remembers feeling embarrassed every time she went to a PTA meeting with her mother. Her mother had remarried and had a different last name. During the interactions with the teachers, her mother was called the wrong name. Today this is very common, but throughout this student's elementary and high school years, she only knew one other person whose parents were divorced. It was awkward and uncomfortable to feel so different.

Textbooks are still limited in their use of people of color. In history class as the story of the settling of the West is told, the Native Americans' contributions to an understanding of ecology are rarely acknowledged. Some high school students are still reading Shakespeare, but rarely read Gabriel Garcia Márquez. Teachers may tell students to "look at me when I talk to you" even though the students' cultural norms may consider this action inappropriate. Sometimes, students may view football players as the school heroes, rather than the gifted scientists, artists, mathematicians, or poets. Femininity is often only defined by the cheerleaders. Middle school girls may want to be scientists, but by the 10th grade, they quit taking advanced science courses. All of these are examples of programmatic patterns that may exist in schools. Just as we must engage in self-reflection to identify who we are and our own biases, we must ask questions about established or institutional biases within the culture of our schools.

How Do Biases Affect Inquiry?

Individuals cannot see what they do not already know. Therefore, it is imperative for culturally responsive educators and leaders of today to implement Step 5, Exploring Programmatic Patterns, and intentionally look for the existence of bias within the programs of schools (see Tool 5.1). Asking questions that go beyond the reported statistics will lead to deeper questions; questions that ask why these students are not enrolling at the same rate as White, middle-class students, for example. Then such inquiry can lead to new questions such as, How can a diverse teacher population be recruited and retained? How can we, as a school staff, ensure academic success for a diverse student population? It is possible that these questions will remain unasked when personal and institutional biases exist.

Tool 5.1 Examining Programmatic Patterns for Bias Within Schools

◆ In what ways is there gender stereotyping at our school?

◆ What do we do at our school to recruit men and women teachers equally?

◆ To what extent do we enforce policies regarding sexual harassment?

◆ To what extent do organizations in our school demonstrate racial or ethnic bias?

◆ To what extent does staff reflect the demographics of the student body? The community?

◆ In what ways do we honor the languages and cultures of the diverse populations in the school?

◆ What types of training do we provide to staff to help them advocate for students from families of poverty?

◆ Who decides what is most important to teach and how it is taught?

◆ What groups are not represented in school organizations?

◆ What does our school do to include all groups?

◆ How can we involve all students in school activities?

◆ How Invitational is our school to all parents?

◆ Are we aware of stereotyping in educators' conversations?

Programmatic Examination
That Explores Patterns of Equity

One way to examine programmatic patterns and outcomes related to diversity is to conduct an equity audit. An equity audit allows school leaders to examine school programs for equity in a variety of ways. For example, to examine programs for equity, variables might include special education, gifted and talented education, bilingual education, student discipline, and extracurricular participation. To examine achievement, equity variables might include such items as state achievement test results, benchmark testing, dropout rates, high school graduation tracks, and the Scholastic Aptitude Test (SAT). Scheurich and Skrla (2003) suggested a simple process for educational leaders to follow to address inequities in schools and districts. These steps are:

1. Select an area for examination and disaggregate data collaboratively.

2. Analyze to explore why the pattern of inequity is occurring.

3. Collaboratively devise an appropriate solution.

4. Implement the solution.

5. Monitor the results. (pp. 91–92)

Equity auditors disaggregate data according to ethnicity, socioeconomic status, and gender in order to identify inequities within a school system. In addition, other categories specific to the school community should be examined (e.g., apartment dwellers, student interest groups). Equity audits tend to be user-friendly because the data are already collected and readily available to educators. In Table 5.1, we have provided examples of equity audits that have been conducted in eight schools or districts.

All of these audits were conducted by practicing superintendents, principals, and teachers who were concerned about examining their work for programmatic patterns. In every case, when these educators looked more closely at their programs or policies, their findings identified inequities, which led them to make recommendations to their schools or districts. In every case, these recommendations, when implemented, resulted in greater programmatic equity at these schools. In other words, examining the work goes beyond personal reflection to program reflection, which results in identifying programmatic patterns.

Table 5.1

Examples of Equity Audits Conducted

Problem Investigated - *Data Collection Source*	Findings	Recommendations
GT classes & ethnicity at 1 high school – *TAKS test*	80% population minority; only 25% of GT students were minority	Encourage student self-referral
Career and Technical Education (CATE) by gender in 2 districts – *AEIS report*	72% in nontraditional CATE classes for Females were male; 75% in CATE course for Males were female	Continue to train educators to explain benefits to all students
Placement of special education students in alternative discipline settings – *AEIS report*	Significant placements of students in special education in discipline alternative settings were found	Identify faculty in need of assistance; revise policies
8th grade math & reading scores by discipline referrals & attendance – *AEIS report*	Reading and math scores were lower when attendance referrals and discipline referrals were greater	Tutorials for students and teachers; parent training
Advanced Placement programs and ethnicity in 2 high schools – *AEIS report*	Inequitable number of minority students in program compared with population	Review school policies
Representation of special education students by ethnicity in one district – *AEIS report*	10% of population was African American; 25% of special ed were African American	Create Action Plan
Grade 5 Science TAKS scores by gender in 4 districts – *AEIS report*	Girls' scores lower than boys' scores in rural and suburban districts	Increase focus on science for girls
Academic achievement on state test by student & teacher ethnicity in 3 districts – *AEIS report*	As number of minority teachers increased, achievement gap decreased	Recruit more minority teachers

Note: AEIS is the Academic Excellence Indicator System, a dataset of school performance indicators available to the public. TAKS is the Texas Assessment of Knowledge and Skills, an annual examination that measures students' understanding of curricular objectives.

Summing Up

Examining programmatic patterns is an important component in the Framework for School Improvement. Tool 5.1 provides a list of questions to consider when examining the program patterns at your school. Do not be discouraged when you identify areas that need improvement. Instead, follow the advice of baseball great, Babe Ruth, who said, "Every strike brings me closer to the next home run." We encourage you to explore these questions individually and in study groups as you build and develop a professional learning community at your school.

> **Remember:**
> Improving the work we do includes program reflection that examines programmatic patterns that may reflect institutional bias in schools.

Reflection Questions

1. What programmatic patterns have you examined most recently?
2. What did you find?
3. What did you do to correct the identified inequities?
4. In what ways are you leading the faculty to examine programmatic patterns?
5. What are you doing to encourage those individuals who are resistant to examining programmatic patterns on your campus?
6. What strategies are you using to engage the community in exploring programmatic patterns at school?

Step 6

Examining the Work: Determining Direction

Don't believe what your eyes are telling you. All they show is limitation.
Look with your understanding, find out what you already know,
and you'll see the way to fly.

Richard Bach, author

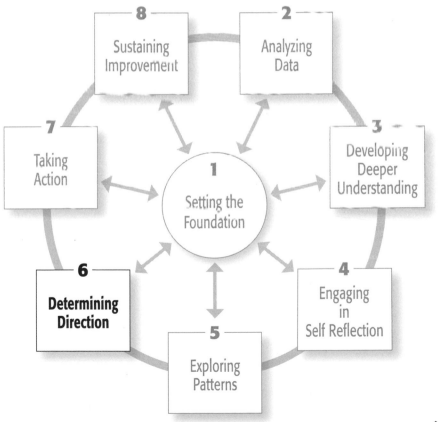

Once you have analyzed data, developed deeper understanding, engaged in self-reflection, and explored patterns, then you and your campus should determine what direction to take. In order to determine a direction, it is important to think about a multitude of important considerations. Deciding what matters most and making the decision as to which path (or paths) to take will be connected to eventual outcomes and performance of the campus. This chapter provides suggestions for how to determine direction for school improvement.

Get Everybody on the Bus

In *Good to Great*, Jim Collins (2001) mentioned that a critical part of success is having the right people doing the right things—everybody is on the same bus in the right seats. One important part of determining direction is building a collaborative team and reaching consensus on the direction and actions necessary to improve. At the basis of such collaboration is trust, which was highlighted in Chapter 1, Setting the Foundation. Many experts agree that to accomplish important tasks, leaders need to involve as many school community members (e.g., teachers, students, parents) as possible. Realistically, not everyone in the school community can serve on the decision-making or improvement committee; however, by using some of the strategies in Chapters 2 and 3 for collecting data, diverse opinions and perspectives can be considered when determining direction and planning specific actions.

We believe that it is especially important to involve teachers when you determine a direction for school improvement. This sort of buy-in from teachers is related directly to the ultimate success of the outcomes. The saying that "two heads are better than one" is especially true in schools. Involving various stakeholders and constituencies, especially teachers, in your planning and decision processes serves many important purposes. Such genuine involvement allows teachers to feel valued and to see that you as the leader value their input. If you want teachers' support for a plan and their cooperation in its implementation, then you need to ensure they are involved with the early idea phases of developing the plan. This also allows you and the improvement team to gain perspective as to what various groups on campus might think or need to make the plans work. Consensus means that most people agree and can support the decision; it does not mean that *everyone* is in total agreement. Developing consensus is a leadership skill covered in other available books and resources. We recommend that school leaders facilitate the process of consensus and practice the skill with teachers. Tool 6.1 is provided as a strategy in building consensus.

How Priorities Are Established

There are many different ways that priorities are established in schools and districts. We review two common ways that priorities are established for schools—externally and internally. Most school leaders are accustomed to having priorities established for them and their schools. State departments, school boards, and central office staff determine direction in a variety of areas using policies, standard practices, and directives. For example, in one school district, school improvement teams were required to document efforts to identify more students from diverse backgrounds for gifted and talented programs. Another way that priorities can be established is in reaction to external events, such as the tragedy of September 11, 2001. In the weeks following, this event made school safety a huge priority for school districts across the country, regardless of what other priorities they might already have set for the school year. Even public opinion can influence priorities, as was the case when character education programs were added in response to public opinions polls. Performance indicators like low test scores might be the source of a school's priorities, as could federal mandates including No Child Left Behind and the accountability requirements included in this legislation. Meeting AYP (Adequate Yearly Progress) and/or improving RtI (Response to Intervention) are other examples of priorities that are established by external forces. Certainly, there is no shortage of externally focused priorities!

Another way to set priorities is a bottom-up approach from the school community—finding out what is important to the members of a school and working to build a consensus for determining the direction of the school's improvement efforts. Because there are so many externally set priorities, sometimes the importance of internal decision making is pushed aside. However, we believe that a combination of both externally and internally focused priorities is important to consider and balance when determining direction. Using the tools discussed in Chapter 3, "Developing Deeper Understanding," leaders can learn about what priorities are important to others in the school community by using surveys, town hall meetings, or even something as simple as a suggestion box. In addition, faculty meetings and parent-teacher organizational meetings are another venue to gather input and to

Tool 6.1 Developing Consensus Building Skills

Instructions

- ◆ Ask participants to stand up and form a line across the room.

- ◆ Introduce the question "Where do you stand?" on the issue of interest.

- ◆ Define what point of view each end of the line represents.

- ◆ Ask participants to move to a point on the line based on their opinion.

- ◆ Instruct participants to talk to those around them about why they chose their positions.

- ◆ Facilitate a discussion about the line; ask those at the extremes to voice their positions there as well as others on the line.

- ◆ Underlying values and beliefs will emerge from the discussion. Often individuals at the extremes will relate to the same values. It is beneficial to discuss these similarities and then allow individuals to align themselves a second time.

Example Question

- ◆ There is much debate over the emphasis placed on standardized testing in schools today.

- ◆ Where do you stand on the need for standardized testing in our school?

- ◆ Please line up at the most appropriate place on the line according to your beliefs about standardized testing.

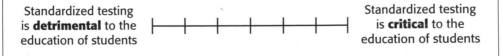

Where do you stand?

| Standardized testing is **detrimental** to the education of students | |————|————|————|————|————|————| | Standardized testing is **critical** to the education of students |

priorities. A bottom-up approach, where people who are vested in the campus have significant input into what issues become priorities, is an excellent way to be sure that initiatives on your campus have support from teachers, parents, students, or other key groups.

Leadership Decisions Needed Before Determining Direction With Others

Before involving others in the process of determining direction, the leader should take a few preliminary steps. First, one should determine which externally set priorities are mandatory and gather necessary information to be able to communicate these priorities to the school. By preparing to discuss such externally set activities, the leader is able to keep his/her staff focused on how these activities might be accomplished rather than why or how someone else decided these were important.

Second, the leader needs to determine which priorities, both from external and internal sources, are not negotiable. Typically, these are issues dealing with compliance, equity, and access for all students and these must be addressed. It is critical for the leader to be clear on negotiable and non-negotiable priorities, as staff will resent the time invested in collaboration on non-negotiable issues. A sure-fire way to destroy trust is to ask people for their opinions when in fact you already have the answer! By being clear on the boundaries of the specific decisions that can be made by you and your team, you will be able to focus resources more efficiently.

Determining Direction

After the leader has determined the priorities that must be addressed, then the campus or improvement team can be involved in deciding on other priorities and ways to accomplish these. Following are some considerations for determining direction:

1. Revisit previous goals and priorities. By reviewing previous goals and priorities, the leader and the team can determine which should remain as priorities. Perhaps previous goals, although still relevant, need to be modified. Making modifications is usually easier than trying to make an old plan fit with new goals or vice versa—think square peg, round hole—it just doesn't fit. In addition, take time to recognize the strengths and successes so that the team can build on what has worked and identify why it might have been successful.

2. Determine areas where more information is needed. Sometimes, more information is needed to determine a direction. Again, remember from previous chapters the importance of collecting and analyzing a variety of data sources. You want to be sure that the data can provide answers for both the "what" and the "why" so that you can determine a direction. Sometimes the direction needed is that your school should collect more information!

3. Recognize limitations. Talented leaders know when they have enough information to make decisions and they execute decisions with almost perfect timing. You may have to help your staff or improvement team understand that they will never have *all* the data or information to determine a direction. By recognizing the limits of time and available data, the team will be able to move forward with a plan of action. It is also important to point out that you all have a finite number of resources, including personnel, money, and time, so realistically every goal cannot be accomplished. As a leader, you will need to verbally recognize such limits and then ask questions such as, What is most important? What are the non-negotiables? What information is essential and what is not? What can wait until next year, or at least until more pressing goals have been reached?

Application/Example of Determining Direction

In this section, we present a process for determining direction. The following list includes issues that have been identified by an improvement team as areas that might be priorities for the school. These were developed after analyzing data, developing deeper understanding, and exploring patterns. In addition, the school leader added several items. Some of these are local concerns; others are federal mandates, district priorities, and school-developed initiatives.

1. adequate yearly progress (AYP)
2. response to intervention (RtI)
3. continue to support low teacher turnover rates and explore reasons why teachers choose to return each year (to build on this strength)
4. over-identification of certain ethnic groups in special education

5. discrepancie

6. attendance

7. school safet

8. extracurricu

9. character ed

10. staff develop

11. implementat

12. parent invol

13. reading improvement strategies

It will be virtually impossible, and certainly unrealistic, for a school team to make all of these top priorities. They are all important areas and each deserves merit. So, how should the leader proceed with determining a direction? First, you have to determine which items have been externally established as priorities for your campus. Next, take the remaining items to your staff—either the entire staff or a representative group, such as the school improvement team, a grade-level council, or a group of department heads—and use a process to decide which priorities are most important. One way to do this is to assign each area on the list to a person or group, who will then research that topic and present the topic to the group at a scheduled date. After each group makes its presentation, faculty or team members would select the areas that should be given highest priority. One time-efficient process to use to gather input from each individual would be to place posters titled with each area around the room. Next, provide each faculty member with three to five dots to vote on the three to five activities that are the most important priorities for the school. At the conclusion of the activity, priorities will be displayed visually. At that point, you and the improvement team can review the areas, enlist further discussion if needed, and decide how many priorities can be managed. Once the direction has been determined, these priorities will be drafted into goals, which will be discussed in the next chapter, Taking Action for School Improvement.

Managing Multiple Priorities

It is important to keep in mind that the priorities of the organization and the time available to achieve the priorities are essentially a mathematical equation: when something is added, it is likely that something else should be subtracted to maintain a balance. In other words, if you simply pile on more priorities, then your equation for getting things accomplished is out of balance. Selective abandonment is a practice that we recommend—deliberately deciding to abandon some projects, putting others on hold, and/or extending the timeline on some priorities.

Realistically, not every priority can be important and urgent. In fact, having too many priorities results in few accomplishments, for these multiple priorities limit the teachers' abilities to focus on what is important. For example, if the district-level office sets goals for your campus, and these priorities are mandatory, then it is possible that you will not be able to satisfy these central office goals and still have time to accomplish many of the goals established by your campus team. This is where plans lose their importance and potency—when they become someone else's plan (such as central office's plan). These plans often become meaningless to campus staff, resulting in little buy-in and a lowered sense of team accomplishment and ownership. When there are too many priorities, you might find yourself and the teachers going through the motions, filling out reports, and attending the meetings. Improvement just becomes one more thing to do—like a hamster on a wheel—lots to do and very busy, but not really moving forward or going anywhere. Try not to let your staff or campus be stuck on the wheel—even the hamster knows when to get off.

Managing the priorities of others is certainly a challenge for school leaders who are often caught in the middle of the needs of students, teachers, and district-level initiatives. Even when the district-level office establishes many of the priorities for your campus, we still advise that you find a way to allow your staff to select a one or two priorities for your campus.

When faced with multiple priorities, it might help to use Covey's (1989) concept of the four quadrants for describing issues or activities.

◆ Along one continuum is the level of importance—is an issue very important, somewhat important, or not very important at all?

◆ Along the other continuum is the sense of urgency—is this an immediate issue or can it be resolved over a longer period of time?

- With these two axes, plot your priorities—which ones are of high importance and high urgency?

- Which ones are important but not very urgent—priorities that can wait?

Following this process should help you determine what to do first. We have provided an example in Tool 6.2.

Summing Up

Determining direction can be particularly challenging for school leaders and their improvement teams. Many schools' improvement efforts are diminished because educators have difficulty balancing multiple priorities. In this chapter, we provided a few ways to encourage the participation of teachers, students, and parents in a genuine process. Although most school leaders are accustomed to having priorities established for them and their schools, we believe that balancing externally and internally focused priorities is important when determining direction. To do so, the leader should determine which priorities are not negotiable by their teams. In addition, the leader should review previous goals and accomplishments and determine where more information may be needed before a direction can be established. To involve others, leaders should learn how to facilitate consensus and practice the skill with groups. One time-efficient strategy to collect the priorities from a large group of teachers was shared. Proactive leaders use a variety of leadership strategies to help their school improvement teams determine direction.

> **Remember:**
> Not everything can be a priority.
> Facilitate consensus to determine direction.

Tool 6.2 Prioritizing Campus Improvement Needs

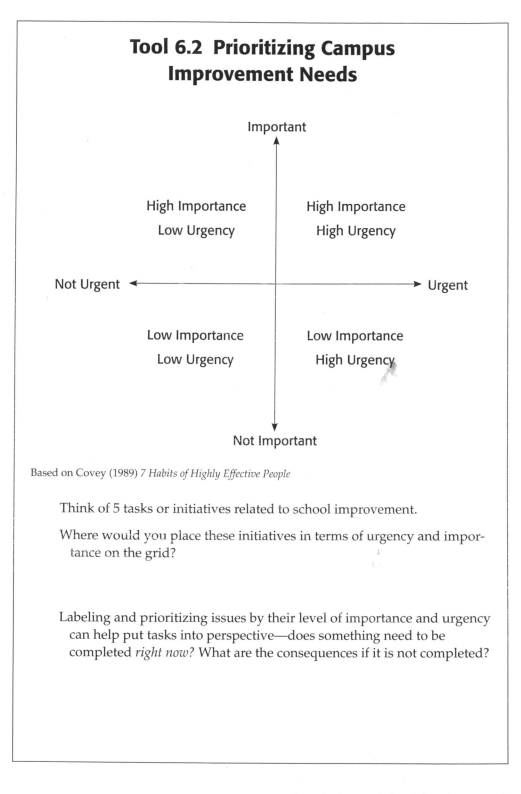

Important

High Importance
Low Urgency

High Importance
High Urgency

Not Urgent ← → Urgent

Low Importance
Low Urgency

Low Importance
High Urgency

Not Important

Based on Covey (1989) *7 Habits of Highly Effective People*

Think of 5 tasks or initiatives related to school improvement.

Where would you place these initiatives in terms of urgency and importance on the grid?

Labeling and prioritizing issues by their level of importance and urgency can help put tasks into perspective—does something need to be completed *right now?* What are the consequences if it is not completed?

Reflection Questions:

1. How were the priorities for your campus selected last year?

2. To what extent can you or your teachers name the current priorities of your school?

3. Think of several issues that might be a priority for your campus.

4. Where would you place these issues on Covey's importance/urgency chart?

5. What does this placement mean to you in terms of dealing with this topic?

6. How do you decide if this topic is truly a priority?

Step 7

Examining the Work: Taking Action for School Improvement

A little learning is a dangerous thing but a lot of ignorance is just as bad.
Bob Edwards, Journalist, Author

There are no secrets to success. It is the result of preparation, hard work, and learning from failure.
Colin Powell, U.S. Secretary of State (2001-2005)

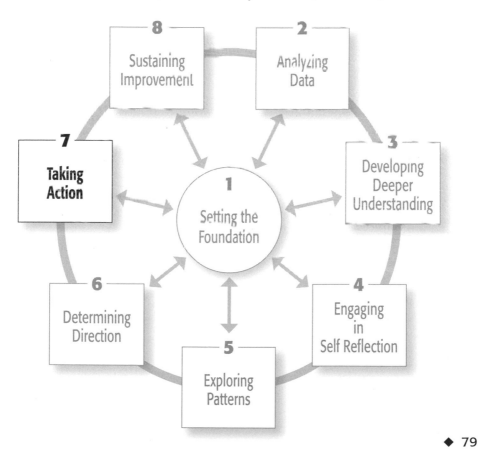

To this point, you have focused on identifying the strengths and target areas for your school or organization by asking a variety of questions. First, you established the foundation for school improvement on your campus. Then you analyzed data reports of key indicators of school success. From these initial reports, you described relevant observations and moved into developing a deeper understanding of the data. You continued to ask additional questions, each requiring more data. You engaged in self-reflection and considered the limited perspectives and biases you may have or have had. In addition, you thought about how your organization unintentionally may be promoting organizational biases by looking for programmatic patterns. After combining all of these findings, you have prioritized the needs and established a direction. This chapter will help you move from ideas and analysis to implementation and action. Step 7 in the Framework for Examining School Improvement is about *Taking Action* and includes organizing and writing a plan of action, and then monitoring and evaluating the activities.

You will be encouraged to begin the process of committing the priorities and ideas to a written plan and establishing a practice that allows for regular examination of progress. For those of you required to submit a written plan to your supervisors, your school board, or community, it is possible that few instructions were given in how to complete this project. Even if you were given a template or form, limited direction may have been given on how the ideas make their way to the page. On the other hand, if you are not required to submit a written or formalized plan of future actions, we recommend that you commit your decisions to a format suggested in this chapter. By doing so, you will provide your staff with direction that can be monitored and reevaluated. Over time, written plans can provide a history of activities and results. Should you be challenged related to your job performance or questioned about the outcomes of your school, these plans can demonstrate your commitment to examining your work.

One underlying assumption of the actions described in Step 7, Taking Action for Improvement, is that actively and genuinely involving staff members and other stakeholders is both beneficial and essential to the success of continuous improvement. Although involving others in the development and monitoring of the plan will require additional time in preparation and meetings, those serious about improvement will accept this as a condition of authentic improvement.

Organizing the Work: Action Committees

Before the actual plan development can occur, a system for organizing the work and the workers is needed. This section of the chapter will help you think about how to manage the process. Working from a committee and subcommittee structure, you will be able to invite staff members to participate actively in continuous improvement. Even if someone who has authority over you provides you with a scripted plan or specifies exactly what your written plan will include, we believe that you should find a way to create campus-level ownership in top-down systems.

In Chapter 1, we described improvement committees and provided ideas for structuring these committees. To review, a committee with approximately 8 to 12 members who will agree to serve as committee leaders is ideal. Staff members of the improvement committee will then be asked to lead or co-lead a subcommittee consisting of a small group of teachers, ranging in size from 3 to 12 members. Ideally, the subcommittees will meet at least once a quarter and sometimes more, depending on the activities for which they lead. School administrators and teachers may be challenged finding time for these meetings. One strategy that has worked is to provide time for these small group meetings during a 20- to 30-minute segment at monthly faculty meetings and during a 1- to 2-hour period within a staff inservice day. For best results, the principal or designated school leader will need to plan the committees and the meeting dates in advance. By sharing the lists of committee members and meeting dates at the beginning of the year, the leader communicates the importance of improvement.

Although there are many benefits to using small groups, involving these groups can be a risk for the school leader. A focus on examination and improvement might imply weakness to some, and positive public relations are vital. Still, parents, students, and community members, well informed, can be some of the most credible supporters as they often have the most accurate information. If you are reluctant to involve members outside of your staff, start small, and invest time to explain how your school examines its practices and programs. Typically, being transparent about the school's improvement process results in community trust. Transparency about the school's improvement processes also builds confidence in you and your teachers' efforts.

Organizing the Work: Action Planning

Written plans of a school's activities to improve specific areas will vary in content and in format. States or local agencies may dictate topics that must be addressed in the plan. Some mandated topics we have had to include as school administrators have been student achievement in each content area, character education, school safety, drug prevention, and teacher training. In fact, in one school district, we have seen the required improvement plan expand from 15 to 55 pages in a 5-year period! School leaders face several practical problems when the improvement plan is filled with mandated activities. It can be difficult to create much campus ownership or meaningful improvement when others are telling you what you need to do. Although we advocate a bottom-up, campus-created approach to improvement, we recognize the realities. Still, we believe that you can authentically examine your work and find meaning and purpose in improvement. A first step will be to find out the requirements so that you understand the parameters of your work.

Should your school have freedom in selecting a way to document your proposed activities, there are several ways to organize your work. Consider a structure that will help segment the topic areas of the plan and work best for your campus. One common framework that has been used by many schools originates from the campus, district, or state goals for education. For example, each selected goal becomes a subheading of the plan, resulting in campus-based objectives and strategies or activities designed for progress toward the goal. If using goals as a framework is not an option, other ideas could be subject areas, competencies, or programs. For example, the components of a plan could be the selected content areas (e.g., math, science, technology, fine arts, reading), extra- or cocurricular programs, school climate/environment, community involvement, and special populations (e.g., special education, bilingual) In addition to the established parts of the plan, different topics can be added and deleted depending on the priorities of the campus.

For example, one school used the following goals to organize its plan:

1. Provide a challenging curriculum.
2. Assess individual student learning and provide support to ensure the academic progress of every student.
3. Provide a safe, orderly, and caring learning environment.
4. Communicate with and involve the school community.
5. Meet the needs of students with special needs.

After the school agreed upon its goals, the principal met with the improvement team and asked members to select one of the five goal areas. Two members were appointed as co-leaders of each area and then faculty at the school provided feedback for committee preferences. These subcommittees of school staff were responsible for making sure the specific actions in their section of the plan occurred. The subcommittee leaders also provided updates at regular improvement committee meetings. As a result, the school made progress toward its goals in ways that distributed the work, encouraged buy-in, and promoted teacher leadership.

Writing a Plan of Action

Although a written plan is not necessary to participate in continuous improvement and to take action, putting your plans in writing helps keep your school focused. Writing the plan helps you achieve clarity about what it is that will focus your efforts. A written plan communicates to the staff and others that to which your school and resources are committed. So, who, then, should write the plan? The improvement committee and/or each subcommittee might draft an action plan for each area. The principal might want to write the plan or ask another school leader to help. Regardless of who puts the drafted plan on paper, it is important that the ideas in the plan result from the input of the entire school, as described in Chapter 6, Determining Direction. Before the final draft is accepted, it is important that the principal or the one who has the "big picture" ensures that the plan is realistic and aligned according to district or state agency requirements.

The format of the plan varies from school to school. Tool 7.1 is available as a suggested format if needed. This template can be altered to fit the needs of your campus; however, the basic components of most plans are action steps (e.g., strategies, activities), person(s) responsible, timelines, resources, and evaluation. We have worked with some plans that require the goals to be written as measurable objectives. There are many variations and specific terminology (e.g., goals, objectives, strategies) used in action planning. Regardless, the main idea is that you and your school know what you plan to do (e.g., improve reading scores, reduce truancy rates).

The action steps or activities in the first column of the template will be tasks to be completed. These tasks should be related to established priorities or goals. For example, action steps to improve reading scores could be setting up a tutorial program or improving the assessment system used to monitor

Tool 7.1 Action Planning Template

Goal:

Action Step(s)	Person(s) Responsible	Timeline: Start/End	Needed Resources	Evaluation
1.				
2.				
3.				

students' progress. The person(s) responsible will be the names or positions of individuals who might be the best to see that the activity is completed. One suggestion is for the subcommittee members in charge of the activity to list several of their names to indicate responsibility, as this committee will be monitoring the progress of this action item. This does not mean that this person is to do all the work but only to see that the described actions are carried out. Sometimes, individuals serving as counselors, administrators, or support staff will be mentioned several times as the designated responsible person. In the third column of the template is the timeline for the action item, which indicates when the activity begins and ends. Even if the action item is something that the school will continue to do after the school year concludes, each item needs an ending date to ensure that evaluation occurs. Activities can be carried over and revised from year to year should they remain as priorities of the school.

After the activities, persons responsible, and timelines are established, think about what is needed to carry out the activity or action item. Resources will be listed in the fourth column. These resources may include time, people, money, equipment, or other types of support. Sometimes the resources will be financial in nature, which can then be connected to the campus budget. Sometimes the resources will involve people, such as the need for additional training or even personnel.

Finally, the evaluation component should be specified in the last column. Questions that can guide the selection of the evaluation for the action item are:

- How will we know that we have completed this activity?

- What types of documentation do we collect that will provide evidence about this activity?

- What types of information will we need to determine if progress has been made?

Consider specific ways to evaluate the outcomes of each activity. Some examples might be attendance records, special program data, referrals, scores, meeting agendas, and classroom observations. By planning these specific five components of an action plan (steps, persons responsible, timeline, resources, and evaluation), you and your team are taking action for improvement.

Monitoring Improvement Actions

A critical part of implementing any successful plan is monitoring its progress. To what extent is the action plan working? What needs to be modified for current circumstances? These formative evaluation and monitoring processes are vitally important to the overall success and progress of school improvement. You need to schedule specific times to have meetings to discuss the progress of the plan. For example, you might want to have a progress meeting every other month, at the end of each quarter, or at the midyear point. Regardless of the actual time span, these meetings should be scheduled for the specific purpose of reviewing action items and progress. When scheduling these meetings, think about what information needs to be reviewed and how long the meeting should last. With these important considerations in mind, plan for enough time to cover everything that is necessary but not so much time that the meetings are overly burdensome for committee members. A meeting agenda will be a helpful planning and communication tool.

Another important part of monitoring the plan includes regular progress reports. This involves the implementation of a system for progress reporting, with a timeline for submitting progress reports and a specific format for what these reports should include. Progress can be reported in a written or oral format, but the reports do need to contain enough information for you and the improvement team to monitor the implementation. As part of the monitoring process, formative assessments should answer the following questions:

- Will the activities still work as planned?

- Do any of the activities need to be altered?

- Have any of the timelines, needed resources, or persons responsible changed?

To answer these questions, data are collected informally on an ongoing basis. These data can include discussions with students, observations in classrooms, or even new directions from the district or state.

One strategy is to ask the team leaders of each subcommittee, which was established in the initial planning stages, to prepare a status update for each activity in their section and to report on these action items at meetings. These leaders and subcommittees can be charged with monitoring progress of certain components on a regular basis, including the provision of both written and verbal reports. E-mail communication and regular check-ups on a periodic basis are also good tools for monitoring progress between meetings. You might have access to an electronic management system to use for monitoring, communication, and updates. When using subcommittees, you as the campus or program leader should have regular communication with the person in charge of each committee. Communication should be ongoing in order to maintain accountability and ownership with the action items.

When setting up progress meetings and producing reports, there might be (probably will be) a great amount of information. Having a committee review all of this information can be very time consuming and might take longer than is reasonable. For this reason, the committee can be divided into groups, and each group can give a brief status report for 5 minutes, with additional time and opportunities for questions at the end. Based on the timeline for the meeting, focus can be given to various activities and components of the improvement plan as appropriate.

If the progress monitoring shows that changes need to be made, what guidelines will be used to make alterations? Is there ever a case where you stick with the original plan no matter what? Does the school district have guidelines for altering documented plans? If changes are needed, the original planning committee should be involved in designing these changes. If many changes are needed, you might need to evaluate the original planning process. Was too much planned? Were priorities not established clearly? Answering these questions is important to avoid similar problems with future planning. If there was too much planned, do you adjust to meet the needs of situation? Overplanning is common, as is being committed to too many priorities. Perhaps some tasks can be started one year and continued or carried over to the next year. Likewise, external forces can result in a need to change the focus of a plan as well, such as an EEOC (Equal Employment Opportunity Commission) compliance visit, a building fire, or even a hurricane.

Evaluating the Action Plan

At the end of each plan year (or whatever timeframe is used), an evaluation will need to be performed. If the plan was implemented for an academic calendar year, as is typically the case for many school improvement efforts, then an evaluation should ideally be conducted before the school year ends. In addition, the evaluation might be performed during the summer months if the committee members are willing to do so or are compensated for their work.

In contrast to the monitoring process, which involves formative assessments, the evaluation of the plan requires summative evaluation to consider what worked and what did not. At this point, it is wise to combine several of the evaluation components for individual activities into a collective survey or interview, in order to avoid 15 different mini evaluations. You can also use evaluation tools that can help gather information for future planning and for needs assessments. This summative process should actually be part of a cycle, which will lead to the creation of new goals and directions, based on evidence found during this process.

The summative evaluation should involve the combination of quantitative and qualitative sources of data, both of which were discussed in Chapters 2 and 3. If the action-planning template was followed (Tool 7.1), then the evaluation components and necessary data have been specified. Additional data may be used in a summative evaluation such as the following: test scores, attendance records, special program data, referrals, technology-usage data, teacher evaluation conferences, interviews, open-ended surveys, and parent meetings. When compiling these data, think about information you already have that could be relevant and would be appropriate to include in a summative report. In reviewing the various data sources for themes, consider both what is provided and what might be missing.

We offer a final consideration of evaluating improvement—sharing results with teachers and the larger school community. Typically, one challenge is that of timing as many evaluations take place at the end of school. If the evaluation is not completely positive, will people feel blamed or responsible for goals that were not met? How can you depersonalize the results and build a sense of shared accountability? Referring to the trust concepts presented in Chapter 1, how you communicate the results will influence people's attitudes and motivations for future action. Leaders who are skilled at building consensus and communicating vision report results in a way that motivates individuals and the team. These leaders assume responsibility and do not blame others; they identify their part in the problems and progress. In addition, they invite the staff to reflect and continue to recognize genuinely the efforts of others.

As the leader, you should think about how to use the evaluation data. To what extent will this information influence the direction of the campus for the upcoming year? How can this information be used to move forward and plan for the following year? Regardless of whether an evaluation reveals exciting results or areas for improvement (typically it is both), it will be important to use these data for the next planning cycle. In fact, the evaluation should help the improvement team answer the questions, "What should we keep on doing?" and "What should we change?"

Summing Up

In this chapter, we outline a way for school leaders and improvement teams to move from ideas and analysis to implementation and action. We recommend that you commit actions to a written format that allows for planning, monitoring, and evaluating. By doing so, you will provide your staff with direction that can be communicated with clarity. To develop and monitor improvement activities, a structure of team leaders assigned to subcommittees was suggested. A critical part of implementing any successful plan is monitoring its progress. Scheduled meetings should be planned to review action items. In addition to the monitoring process, a summative evaluation of the action items should be conducted to determine what worked and what did not.

In addition to planning and monitoring action items, the leader should consider how to communicate progress and results. Communication of negative outcomes might result in discouraged and unmotivated students and teachers. Leaders should avoid blaming others but rather identify their roles in both the problems and progress. Implementing positive actions that have been considered carefully results in improved schools.

Remember:
An important part of Taking Action for School Improvement is the continuous monitoring of progress.

Reflection Questions:

1. Organizing: What are the structures already in place for improvement activities? How much flexibility do you have as a school leader in your organization? What are some of the external forces for you and your campus?

2. Monitoring: What will be your system for monitoring the progress of each action item? What are the specific meeting dates for progress monitoring?

3. Evaluation: How will you evaluate your performance? How will you use these findings for further planning and improvement? How will you communicate these findings?

Step 8

Examining the Work: Sustaining Improvement

We are made wise not by the recollection of our past, but by the responsibility for our future.

George Bernard Shaw, Irish playwright

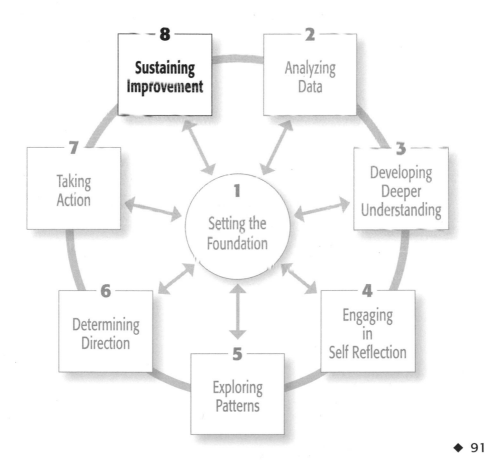

Recently, MetLife Foundation and the National Association ary School Principals (NASSP) announced the names of 10 schools designated as Breakthrough Schools, schools that are "dramatically improving student achievement" in poverty areas across the nation ("MetLife and NASSP Name 2009 Breakthrough Schools," 2009, p. 1). Mel Riddile, who leads the NASSP National Center for High School Leadership, commented that the driving force behind these schools is "an unwavering commitment to school improvement" ("MetLife and NASSP," 2009, p. 1). Sharon Johnson, principal of Withrow University High School, one of the Breakthrough Schools, commented that success is possible for every student.

In that same issue of the NASSP *NewsLeader*, Gerald Tirozzi, executive director of NASSP, stressed the importance of improving the graduation rate and giving all students an opportunity to go to college. He reminded school leaders that in order for these goals to be achieved, "we cannot wait until high school to begin that work" (Karhuse, 2009, p. 3). Committing to school improvement for all students, believing that success is possible, improving the graduation rate, and increasing the opportunity for all students to go to college means that educators must focus on sustaining improvements. However, as leaders examine their work for school improvement and are committed to sustaining improvements, at the same time, they must be actively engaged in looking to the future. We have labeled Step 8 in the Framework as Sustaining Improvement, but it is essential to understand that improvements cannot be sustained without actively looking to the future. In other words, to not move forward is to move backward.

Gary Marx (2006) identified trends that are predicted to have a profound impact on the future for all of society in these changing times. Although all of the trends he noted are important, some of the more pointed trends for educators include the following:

◆ a shift in the majority/minority groups of the U.S. population

◆ an increase in the availability of technology

◆ an increase in the need for personalization

◆ an increase in the need for consideration of varying points of view

As busy educators stay engaged in the daily work of schooling, it is not enough to keep the focus on improving educational opportunities for their students. In order to sustain improvements, leaders must keep a watchful eye on the future and the impact of futuristic trends for schools.

Strategies for Sustaining Improvement

Schools that have professional learning communities in place are generally already engaged in sustaining improvement and actively building for the future. Learning communities use several strategies for sustaining improvement while at the same time looking futuristically (or forecasting) to prepare for the future. We have already discussed several common strategies to sustain improvement that included using data collection techniques such as the questionnaire, as described in Chapter 3. Questionnaires provide excellent opportunities for gathering information and opinions quickly. These can be designed specifically to project future needs and goals and to determine which improvement activities should be continued. In this chapter, additional strategies to sustain improvement will be explained—Force Field Analysis, the Delphi method, Nominal Group Technique, and the CARE model.

Force Field Analysis

Kurt Lewin, a social scientist, believed that there are forces that drive change and forces that resist change. His Force Field Analysis is a tool that has been in use for nearly 70 years. He theorized that in order for change to occur, the driving forces for the change must exceed the resisting forces against the change. Lewin believed that bringing about change begins with understanding the circumstances surrounding the needed change. As educators work to sustain improvements and at the same time build for the future, conducting a Force Field Analysis contributes to informed decision making.

For example, a curriculum director concerned with sustaining recent improvements in the district's technology initiative recently shared an interest in implementing a new technology initiative in her school district. She gathered a district-wide committee of teachers, parents, and administrators and explained the proposed initiative. Using the tool of the Force Field Analysis, she facilitated the group in brainstorming the possible driving and resisting forces of the potential change. Some of the driving forces identified by the staff were (a) the need for students to use technology in authentic ways for future postsecondary success, (b) the commitment made by a majority of teachers to participate in extended training, and (c) the support of the school board in the local district for these changes. Some of the resisting forces were (a) the expense of the initiative, (b) the need for additional personnel

to manage the infrastructure issues, and (c) the lack of parent
to technology and the Internet in students' homes. After com
Field Analysis with her staff, she and the committee developed a p
specified strategies to address the driving and resisting forces.

If your district or school is attempting to make a decision and is concerned about how that decision will affect the future, follow these steps for
conducting a Force Field Analysis:

1. Describe the current situation.
2. Describe the proposed change.
3. Identify what will happen if no change occurs.
4. Identify the forces driving the proposed change.
5. Identify the forces resisting the change.
6. Determine whether the change is viable (this can be done by assign-
   ing points to the forces driving the change and points to the forces
   resisting change).
7. If the change is viable, what is needed for implementation? Will you
   need to reduce the strength of the forces opposing the change, or
   increase the forces driving the change?

For more information about this technique, conduct a search using the
term *Force Field Analysis* or see http://www.mindtools.com.

Delphi Method

While the Delphi method is an excellent tool for developing deeper
understanding, it is also an important strategy for identifying ways to sustain improvement and looking futuristically at school needs. The Delphi
method relies on a panel of experts or people who would be affected by
the decision or change. School leaders implement the Delphi method frequently. It is a relatively painless way to make decisions involving as many
as 20 participants and at the same time provide a level of confidentiality
The participants respond to questionnaires in two or more rounds and often
responses are made electronically with e-mail. After each round, the facilitator provides a summary of the answers given and, when possible, provides
the rationale for those answers. In this way, participants are encouraged to
reconsider and revise earlier answers in light of this collective information
from other members of the group. Generally, as the process continues, the
range of responses decreases and the group converges towards some level
of consensus.

To implement this process in examining and sustaining school improvement, you may want to follow this format:

- Send around a problem statement to staff

- Ask staff to write down what he or she believe needs to be done

- Retrieve the written comments

- Reproduce everyone's comments

- Return all the comments to the participants

- Participants read comments and then individually write a synthesis of the various ideas (this step is optional and often is omitted due to time constraints)

- Collect everyone's syntheses or you do this yourself

- Make a new list of all synthesized ideas

- Send the new list back to participants and ask them to rank items

- Collect and compute an average and frequency of ratings; then return tallies to participants to re-rank.

Nominal Group Technique

The Nominal Group Technique is another way to examine school improvement with an eye on future needs of the school that builds consensus and leads to genuine school improvement. This five-step process is usually done in small group meetings, often at a faculty meeting, with a facilitator leading the conversation. To implement, follow these five steps:

- Have each individual within a small group silently generate and write perceived needs/issues. Do not allow discussion among participants at this point.

- Ask each individual to share orally with the small group one perceived need/issue at a time. The Facilitator then writes these on a flip chart with NO discussion.

- Lead small group discussions of each perceived need/issue for further clarification.

- Ask group members to rewrite and rate all perceived needs/issues listed in the previous step. Numerical values can be assigned to each from 1–5 for example.

When using the Nominal Group Technique, remember that the facilitator must not be judgmental or allow judgmental comments from participants as they work through the issues for clarification

CARE Model

The CARE model is another way to examine improvement with a focus on sustainability (keeping the good things we are doing) while building for the future (identifying future concerns). The CARE model emphasizes four components:

♦ Concerns—Look to the future to identify the most important concerns in the school that must change in order to sustain school improvement.

♦ Affirmations—Look to the present to identify the most important affirmations or positive structures/policies at school that must be sustained.

♦ Recommendations—Recommendations based on identified Concerns and Affirmations should be implemented that are SMART: specific, measurable, attainable, relevant, and timely.

♦ Evaluations—Commit to conducting regular evaluations. List the specific ways that the recommendations will be implemented (e.g., walk-throughs, surveys, assessments, reflective conversations, group discussions).

Too often educators focus so exclusively on what needs to change that they lose perspective on what does not need to change in the process. However, as circumstances change in a school community, school improvement cannot be sustained without making adjustments and changes with the future in mind. Consider the school that has received strong affirmations from community leaders for its visible teacher and leader presence in the community. What might happen if this school decided to buy into the technology movement so strongly that it no longer sustained and maintained these strong community ties? Participating in a CARE model examination encourages this school faculty to work toward addressing those needed technology concerns while at the same time sustaining its strong community presence. In other words, while working to address concerns we must continue to maintain that which we do well. In this way we sustain improvement while building for the future.

The CARE model is included for you as Tool 8.1. This and other strategies mentioned in this chapter can be done individually or in small or large groups. Engage your staff in examining the work you do to improve schools with an eye on the future.

The Challenge to Examine Ways to Improve Schools

In a recent report, Loveless (as cited in Bracey, 2009) reported that students enrolled in eighth-grade Algebra courses were functioning at a second-grade level in math according to NAEP (National Assessment of Educational Progress) assessments. Because most educators agree that Algebra is a gateway to college, the placement of children in Algebra in the eighth grade could become an issue of equity and fairness. In fact, in the past 20 years, policies placing eighth graders into Algebra classes have doubled the percentage of students enrolled in advanced mathematics. Yet, Bracey (2009) has argued that many of these children are "misplaced" and that too often this policy results not only in leaving children behind, but "in over their heads" (p. 57). He suggested that the solution is not to lose sight of the goal to hold all children to high standards, but instead to emphasize learning, not course taking. This is an example of how sustaining improvement and building for the future are so closely connected. Certainly, practices that double the percentage of eighth graders taking Algebra classes are worth sustaining. However, examining this process with an eye to the future is important to ensure that these practices are implemented in such a way that students are successful. For example, tutoring might need to be in place in order to maintain not just placement but student academic growth. It is critical that educators continuously examine school improvement and work toward the goal of increasing student achievement for all students.

Schools are changing every day based on a myriad of circumstances that are occurring in the United States and globally. It is imperative that educators have knowledge of other world cultures as the world becomes "smaller" based on technological and media advances. Moreover, economic structures are changing. For example, a predicted 2 million children will lose their homes due to economic crises in the United States. Moreover, the U.S. Department of Agriculture indicates that children who suffered a substantial disruption in food availability nearly doubled from 430,000 in 2006 to

Tool 8.1 CARE Model: Planning Tool

Identify Concerns that must change (look to the future)

(Assign points to concerns from 1 to 3 in the order of the most important issues to consider.)

1. _____
2. _____
3. _____

Identify Affirmations that must be sustained (look to the present)

(Assign points to affirmations from 1 to 3 in the order of the most important issues to consider.)

1. _____
2. _____
3. _____

SMART Recommendations that must be implemented:
(Specific, Measurable, Attainable, Relevant, Timely)

(Assign points to recommendations from 1 to 3 in the order of the most important recommendations to implement.)

1. _____
2. _____
3. _____

EVALUATE – Specifically and Often

(Identify the best ways to evaluate the implemented recommendations.)

1. _____
2. _____
3. _____

691,000 in 2007 ("Foreclosed: 2 Million," 2009). These and many other issues have an incredible impact on the lives of students. School improvements are most likely to be sustained when educators also look to the future to provide needed structures for these improvements to continue.

Summing Up

We believe that the Framework for Examining School Improvement embeds the necessary components for school leaders to analyze and implement actions that lead to improved schools. Our Framework uses 8 steps that are cyclical and continuous. Step 1, Setting the Foundation, forms the basis for all improvement activity. This step emphasizes having a shared vision, understanding the need for inquiry, valuing improvement by providing time, and building trusting relationships. Step 2, Analyzing Data, emphasizes five steps in order to analyze data: prepare, focus, understand, observe, and interpret. Step 3, Developing Deeper Understanding, incorporates strategies for gaining a richer understanding of the school. Step 4, Engaging in Self-Reflection, challenges educators to reflect on three questions: Who am I? What biases do I have? And why am I an educator? Steps 2 through 4 provide strategies that uncover needed information to implement Step 5, Exploring Programmatic Patterns. All of this information is then used in the school improvement process as Step 6, Determining Direction. Once direction has been established, it is time to implement Step 7, Taking Action. When action is taken and school improvement strategies are in place, Step 8, Sustaining Improvement, is critical. This last step goes beyond maintenance strategies to include active planning for the future. Once the 8 steps have been followed, it is time to begin again with Step 1 because examining school improvement is a continuous process. Use Tool 8.2 to check your use of the Framework for Examining School Improvement.

Tool 8.2 Assessing Progress
Framework for Examining School Improvement

- ◆ What am I doing to establish and improve the foundation?

- ◆ How am I involving others in creating a shared vision?

- ◆ Do I understand the need for inquiry?

- ◆ What am I doing to make time for school improvement?

- ◆ What am I doing to build trusting interpersonal relationships?

- ◆ In what ways am I analyzing data?

- ◆ To what extent am I developing deeper understanding?

- ◆ How often do I engage in self-reflection?

- ◆ What programmatic patterns have I discovered at our school?

- ◆ What strategies did I use to determine direction?

- ◆ What actions am I taking for school improvement?

- ◆ What am I doing to sustain improvement?

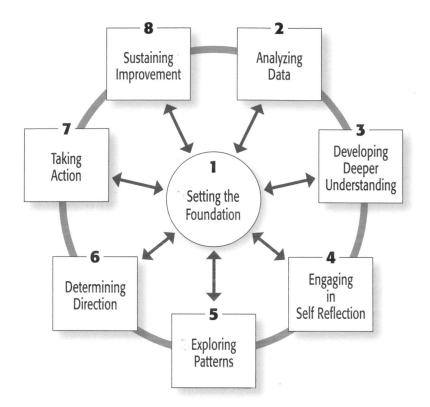

When we examine what we do at school to ensure that the foundation is in place, when we analyze data, when we develop deeper understanding, when we engage in self-reflection, when we explore programmatic patterns, when we determine direction, and when we work to sustain that direction to build a better future for students—we bring about general improvement for schools. We do this because we care, or as the motto for Hallmark Cards says, "When you care enough to send the very best." When we care enough to give our very best, we examine ways to improve schools by investigating everything we do. When we improve schools, we improve the lives of our students, and thus, we improve the future for all of us.

Remember:

As busy educators engaged in the daily work of schooling, we must keep focused on improving educational opportunities for our students. One way to do this is to sustain improvements with an eye to the future.

Reflection Questions:

1. What improvement activities does your school need to sustain?
2. What future issues do you predict might occur at your school?
3. How will these circumstances affect your school?
4. What strategies can you implement to position your school to adequately survive the changing circumstances?
5. Using the CARE Model, what is the most important concern to change at your campus?
6. Using the CARE Model, what is the most important affirmation to sustain at your campus?
7. What recommendations will you implement?
8. How will you evaluate those recommendations?

References

Bennis, W. (1999). Five competencies of new leaders. *Executive Excellence, 16*, 4–5.

Bennis, W., & Goldsmith, J. (1997). *Learning to lead: A workbook on becoming a leader.* (Rev. ed.) Reading, MA: Perseus Books.

Bingham, C. (2001). *Schools of recognition: Identity politics and classroom practices.* Lanham, MD: Rowman and Littlefield.

Bracey, G. W. (2009). Over their heads, out of their league. *Principal Leadership, 9*(5), 56–58.

Bryk, A. S., & Schneider, B. (2002). *Trust in schools: A core resource for improvement.* New York: Russell Sage Foundation.

Collins, J. (2001). *Good to great.* New York: HarperCollins.

Covey, S. (1989). *7 habits of highly effective people: Powerful lessons in personal change.* New York: Free Press.

Darling-Hammond, L. (2007). The flat earth and education: How America's commitment to equity will determine our future. *Educational Researcher, 36*(8), 318–334.

Eisner, E. (2006). The satisfactions of teaching. *Educational Leadership, 63*(6), 44–46.

"Foreclosed: 2 Million Homeless Students and Counting." (2009, January). *NewsLeader, 56*(5), 8.

Howard, G. (1999). *You can't teach what you don't know.* New York: Teachers College Press.

Karhuse, A. (2009, January). Middle level proves to be turning point for college and career readiness. *NewsLeader, 56*(5), 3, 7.

Leithwood, K., & Jantzi, D. (2005). Transformational leadership. In B. Davies (Ed.). *The essentials of school leadership* (pp. 31-43). Thousand Oaks, CA: Corwin.

Marx, G. (2006). *Sixteen trends: Their profound impact on our future.* Arlington, VA: Educational Research Service.

Mead, M. (1966). *Coming of age in Samoa* (3rd ed.). New York: William Morrow & Co.

Merriam-Webster Online Dictionary. (2008). Improvement. Retrieved January 6, 2009, from http://www.merriam-webster.com/dictionary/improvement

MetLife and NASSP Name 2009 Breakthrough Schools. (2009, January). *NewsLeader, 56*(5), 1.

Moore, M. T., & Overberg, P. (2009, May 14). Gap between Boomers, young minorities grows. *USA Today*, 1A.

National Poverty Center. (2008). *Poverty in the United States: Frequently asked questions.* Retrieved December 21, 2008, from http://www.npc.umich.edu/poverty

National Center for Education Statistics. (2005). *NAEP trends.* U.S. Department of Education, National Assessment of Educational Progress. Retrieved August 10, 2007, from http://nces.ed.gov

Nelson, J., Palonsky, S., & McCarthy, M. (2007). *Critical issues in education: Dialogues and dialectics.* Boston: McGraw–Hill.

Orfield, G. (2001). *Schools more separate: Consequences of a decade of resegregation.* Cambridge, MA: Harvard University, Civil Rights Project.

Orfield, G., & Yun, J. T., (1999). *Resegregation in American schools. Civil Rights Project Report.* Cambridge, MA: Harvard University.

Pang, V. (2005). *Multicultural education: A caring-centered, reflective approach* (2nd ed.). Boston: McGraw-Hill.

Rubenstein-Avila, E. (2006). Connecting with Latino learners. *Educational Leadership, 63*(5), 38–43.

Scheurich, J. J., & Skrla, L. (2003). *Leadership for equity and excellence.* Thousand Oaks, CA: Corwin Press.

School Matters. (2006). *Narrowing the achievement gap: Schools in Texas that are making significant progress 2003–04 to 2004–05.* Washington, DC: Standard and Poor's.

Sparks, D., & Loucks-Horsley, S. (1989). Five models of staff development. *Journal of Staff Development, 10*(4), 40–57.

Texas Education Agency. (2005). *Academic Excellence Indicator System.* Retrieved April 26, 2009, from http://ritter.tea.state.tx.us/perfreport/aeis/2005/index.html

Trotter, A. (2001, May 23). Census shows the changing face of U.S. households. *Education Week*, 5.

Notes

Notes

Notes